D1078562

Pocket
ALGARVE

TOP EXPERIENCES · LOCAL LIFE · MADE EASY

Andy Symington

In This Book

QuickStart Guide

Your keys to understanding the region – we help you decide what to do and how to do it

Need to Know
Tips for a smooth trip

Regions
What's where

Explore the Algarve

The best things to see and do, region by region

Top Experiences
Make the most of your visit

Local Life
The insider's region

The Best of the Algarve

The region's highlights in handy lists to help you plan

Best...
Activities and attractions

Best...
Experiences and tips

Survival Guide

Tips and tricks for a seamless, hassle-free experience

Getting Around
Travel like a local

Essential Information
Including where to stay

Our selection of the region's best places to eat, drink and experience:

⊙ **Experiences**

⊗ **Eating**

🍸 **Drinking**

⊛ **Entertainment**

🔒 **Shopping**

These symbols give you the vital information for each listing:

📞	Telephone Numbers	👪	Family-Friendly
🕐	Opening Hours	🐾	Pet-Friendly
🅿	Parking	🚌	Bus
🚭	Nonsmoking	⛴	Ferry
@	Internet Access	Ⓜ	Metro
📶	Wi-Fi Access	Ⓢ	Subway
🌱	Vegetarian Selection	🚊	Tram
📖	English-Language Menu	🚆	Train

Find each listing quickly on maps for each region:

Bar Hemingway

16 🍸 Map p233, B2

Legend has it that Hemi self, wielding a machine rate this timber-pan ered bar during showpiece is a en by Papa ar town. Dress s.com; Hôtel Rit 🕐6.30pm-2a

Lonely Planet's Algarve

Lonely Planet Pocket Guides are designed to get you straight to the heart of the destination.

Inside you'll find all the must-do experiences, plus tips to make your visit to each one really memorable. We've split the region into easy-to-navigate regions and provided clear maps so you'll find your way around with ease. Our expert author has searched out the best of the best: walks, food, nightlife and shopping, to name a few. Because you want to explore, our 'Local Life' pages will take you to some of the most exciting areas to experience the real Algarve.

And of course you'll find all the practical tips you need for a smooth trip: itineraries for short visits, how to get around, and how much to tip the guy who serves you a drink at the end of a long day's exploration.

It's your guarantee of a really great experience.

Our Promise

You can trust our travel information because Lonely Planet authors visit the places we write about, each and every edition. We never accept freebies for positive coverage, so you can rely on us to tell it like it is.

QuickStart Guide **7**

Explore the Algarve **21**

The Best of the Algarve **113**

The Algarve's Best...

Survival Guide **129**

QuickStart Guide

Welcome to the Algarve

A narrow strip of land and sand at Europe's southwestern end, the Algarve is a Mediterranean idyll, with fragrances of pine, rosemary, wine and grilling fish drifting over some absolutely stunning beaches. Only this isn't the Med, it's the Atlantic, so add seriously surfable waves, important maritime history and great wildlife-watching opportunities to the mix. And nightlife? You bet your life...

Beach at Benagil, along the Percurso dos Sete Vales Suspensos (p66)
INAQUIM/GETTY IMAGES ©

The Algarve
Top Experiences

Via Algarviana (p72)

The Algarve's interior is authentic and undeveloped, so what better way to get to know these rolling cork-, pine- and gorse-covered hills than on foot? This trail crosses the region, but offers appealing day walks, too.

Parque Natural da Ria Formosa (p26)

The eastern Algarve coastline is a fragmented affair of lagoons, tidal wetlands and sand islands. It's all encompassed in a natural reserve that offers magnificent ocean beaches, local shellfishing communities and great birdwatching.

Surfing the West Coast (p104)

The Algarve's less-developed west coast is a real paradise. The wonderful sandy beaches are prime destinations for surfers or anybody who appreciates the sound of breakers and the mist of seaspray.

Fortaleza de Sagres (p92)

Occupying a large promontory, this strategically situated fortress offers a great circular walk with superb clifftop perspectives, as well as an insight into military history and perhaps the times of Prince Henry the Navigator.

Cacela Velha (p40)

This perfectly formed little village seems too postcard-pretty to be real, but it is still home to a community of shellfishers. It overlooks a lovely estuary and lonely beaches.

Cabo de São Vicente (p94)

Europe's southwestern-most point is a cliff beyond which the Atlantic stretches wide and lonely. There's an engaging museum here, but it's gazing into the infinite, and the evocative sunsets, that are most memorable.

On the Water (p78)

The summery party town of Lagos is the base for a bewildering array of watery activities, from plumbing the depths with a scuba tank to cruising the ocean spotting dolphins and seabirds.

Faro's Sé (p24)

The centrepiece of Faro's lovely Cidade Velha (Old Town), the *sé* (cathedral) offers a sturdy exterior, an intriguing interior (including a bone chapel) and inspiring vistas from its bell tower.

The Algarve Local Life

Insider tips to help you find the real Algarve

Despite mass tourism and swaths of heavy development, happily it's still relatively easy to hunt out authentic experiences in the Algarve.

Olhão: a Fishing Town (p28)

▶ Fishing heritage
▶ Island beaches

One of the Algarve's important ports, the town of Olhão preserves plenty of fishing character and has one of the region's most architecturally noteworthy markets. There's plenty to explore here, and the town is also a gateway to spectacular island beaches accessible by boat.

Along the Guadiana (p42)

▶ Castles
▶ River views

The Guadiana river divides the Algarve from Spain and its banks make intriguing territory for exploration. Typically for a borderland, there are sturdy fortresses here, and you'll also find good birdwatching, an unpretentious fishing town, hearty inland cuisine and an unusual beach.

Serra do Caldeirão (p52)

▶ Hill villages
▶ Local museums

Despite being only a short drive from the coast, a real taste of traditional Portugal can be had in this area of small villages and undulating landscapes of orchards, cork trees and tough scrubland. It's also great for hiking and birdwatching.

Portimão & Praia da Rocha (p62)

▶ Seafood meals
▶ Lively nightlife

With an important fish-canning history, it's appropriate that the unprettified town of Portimão is one of the Algarve's most enjoyable places to eat seafood. The adjacent beach of Praia da Rocha is more touristy, but has great sand and is very lively on summer nights.

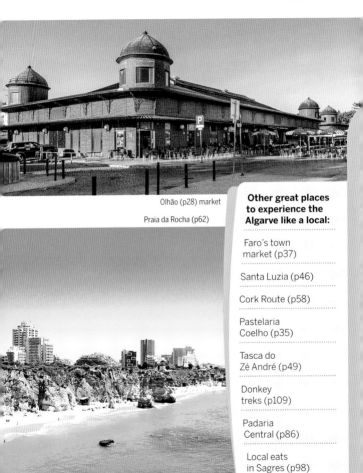

Olhão (p28) market

Praia da Rocha (p62)

Other great places to experience the Algarve like a local:

Faro's town market (p37)

Santa Luzia (p46)

Cork Route (p58)

Pastelaria Coelho (p35)

Tasca do Zé André (p49)

Donkey treks (p109)

Padaria Central (p86)

Local eats in Sagres (p98)

The Algarve
Day Planner

Day One

☀ The Faro region has a good variety of attractions that showcase the history and natural environment of the Algarve. Start your day in the Cidade Velha, the compact and winsome old centre of town. Enter the **cathedral** (p24), climbing the bell tower to gaze out over the area and its offshore estuaries and islands, and pay a brief visit to the **Museu Municipal** (p31) before heading across town to the **Igreja de Nossa Senhora do Carmo** (p31) for a peek at the ghostly beauty of its skull-and-bone chapel.

☀ Contract a boat trip for the afternoon, preferably one of the longer ones, to get a feel for the intriguing landscapes and waterscapes of the **Parque Natural da Ria Formosa** (p26). Alternatively, you could hire a kayak and explore the area yourself.

☽ Station yourself at **O Castelo** (p37) for a sunset drink, then choose from one of Faro's excellent dining options. The Cidade Velha has tourist-oriented but undeniably atmospheric restaurants, including the elegant **Faz Gostos** (p33), while there are friendly, no-frills Portuguese neighbourhood places on the northern edge of central Faro, such as cheap-and-cheerful **Chefe Branco** (p34).

Day Two

☀ The far west of the Algarve offers the chance to escape the tourist beat, see some amazing beaches, and explore Portugal's impressive maritime history: ships sailed from here into the unknown during the country's Age of Discovery. Head first for the **Fortaleza de Sagres** (p92) – part fortress, part invigorating headland walk with sublime coastal views – and then travel the last few kilometres to the end of Portugal at **Cabo de São Vicente** (p94), with its spectacular cliffs and intriguing museum.

☀ In the afternoon wind your way up the west coast, pausing to appreciate some of Europe's finest beaches for those who love surf and spray. Drive or walk the circuit of the two beaches at **Carrapateira** (p107), then check out beaches **Praia de Vale Figueira** (p107) and **Praia da Amoreira** (p107).

☽ If you stay in the quiet, pretty town of Aljezur, head up to the **castelo** (p109) for sunset views, then enjoy a tasty fish dinner at friendly **Pont'a Pe** (p110), one of a handful of unpretentious restaurants. If you're after nightlife, head back to Sagres and hit the strip of surfer-friendly bar-restaurants on **Rua Comandante Matoso** (p100).

Short on time?
We've arranged the Algarve's must-sees into these day-by-day itineraries to make sure you see the very best of the region in the time you have available.

Day Three

Head off early in the morning to **Monchique** (p70), a lovely hill village, and do a half-day walk from here, perhaps climbing to the top of **Fóia** (p75), the highest hill in the Algarve. If you're feeling less energetic, drive up, then spend a couple of hours in the **spa** (p128) at nearby Caldas de Monchique. Have lunch at one of the Monchique restaurants specialising in hearty hill-country cuisine, perhaps the appealingly rustic **A Charrete** (p76).

After lunch, drive down to postcard-pretty Silves, and investigate its sizeable Moorish **castelo** (p65), its Gothic **cathedral** (p65) and the intriguing well in its **Museu Municipal** (p65). Spend some time wandering the narrow streets and the riverside and have a coffee and snack on the terrace of the **Café Inglês** (p67).

Head from Silves to **Lagos** (p78) and prepare yourself for a decent night out. From creative cocktails at **Bon Vivant** (p87) to beer bongs at **the Tavern** (p88), there's enough variety in this always-buzzing town to find something that will suit. There's a thriving restaurant scene here, too; try sandside **Bar Quim** (p86) or stylish **Atlântico** (p85).

Day Four

In the morning head for the hills to investigate the picturesque rural landscapes of the **Serra do Caldeirão** (p52). Visit the charming **Fábrica de Brinquedos** (p53) near Alte, the little museum in **Salir** (p53) and the jewel-like village of **Querença** (p53) before heading back to the coast, perhaps with a brief stop at the fabulous tiled church of **São Lourenço de Matos** (p55), if you can get there by 1pm.

While away the afternoon in **Tavira** (p38), spending time in its interesting **Nucleo Islâmico** (p45) museum, pacing the riverside and exploring the old town. In the late afternoon drive out to utterly charming **Cacela Velha** (p40), a small village overlooking the coastline, at its best (and least busy) in the evening light.

Back in Tavira, settle in to one of the numerous local restaurants for dinner; as everywhere in the Algarve, the fish on offer is especially good. **Casa Simão** (p46) hasn't blown the budget on decor, but offers a family welcome and reliably delicious local meals. What's available afterwards depends a bit on the season, but in summer there are numerous choices. **Tavira Lounge** (p48) is a reliable spot for a well-made mixed drink.

Need to Know

**For more information,
see Survival Guide (p129).**

Currency
Euro (€)

Language
Portuguese; English widely spoken

Visas
EU citizens can stay indefinitely; many other nationals can enter visa free for up to 90 days.

Money
ATMs are widespread. Nearly all accommodation and upper-end restaurants accept credit cards.

Mobile Phones
Roaming charges for EU phones are low or nonexistent. With an unlocked phone, local SIM cards are cheap and have good packages available.

Time
Western Europe Time (GMT/UTC plus zero hours), clocks go forward an hour in late March and back again in late October.

Plugs & Adaptors
Plugs have two round pins; electrical current is 230V.

Tipping
Tipping in restaurants is not expected, but appreciated. Locals leave around 2% to 5%; 10% is generous.

① Before You Go

Your Daily Budget

Budget less than €50
► Dorm bed €15–€25

► Self-catering, or *prato do dia* (daily special) in a cheap restaurant €6–€8

► Inexpensive public transport

Midrange €50–€120
► Double room in a midrange hotel €50–€100

► Dinner for two in a midrange restaurant €25–€50

► Book online to save on accommodation

Top End more than €120
► Boutique hotel room from €120

► Three-course meal in a top restaurant from €40

Useful Websites

Booking.com (www.booking.com) The handiest hotel-booking service for the region, with a useful smartphone app.

Lonely Planet (www.lonelyplanet.com/portugal) Destination information, hotel bookings, traveller forum and more.

Visit Algarve (www.visitalgarve.pt) Official tourism site with handy downloads.

Advance Planning

Several months before If you're coming in July or August, reserve your accommodation now; the earlier, the better.

One month before Book high-end restaurants, tee times at upmarket golf courses and water-park tickets.

One week before Book your kitesurfing lessons, cruises or other water-based activities.

2 Arriving in the Algarve

Most visitors to the Algarve arrive at Faro Airport (FAO; 📞 289 800 800; www.ana.pt; 📶). From the airport, a bus will take you to Faro's transport terminals, where it's easy to hop on a bus or train to access the rest of the region.

✈ From Faro Airport

Destination	Best Transport
Faro	Bus 14 or 16 to central Faro
Lagos	Bus 16 to train station, train to Lagos
Loulé	Bus 16 to bus station, bus to Loulé
Sagres	Bus 16 to bus station, bus to Sagres
Tavira	Bus 16 to train station, train to Tavira

From Lisbon

Destination	Best Transport
Faro	Plane, or train from Gare do Oriente
Lagos	Train from Gare do Oriente
Loulé	Bus from Terminal Rede Expressos
Sagres	Bus from Terminal Rede Expressos
Tavira	Train from Gare do Oriente

✈ At the Airport

Faro Airport The Algarve's main airport is small but fully kitted out for holidaymakers, with several car-hire firms, shuttle-bus and car-transfer services, a multilingual tourist-information office, ATMs, exchange office, free wi-fi (for 30 minutes), an internet terminal, printer, post office, and golf-club hire.

3 Getting Around

Many visitors to the Algarve hire a car, and it's very pleasant to have on-demand air-con and the ability to stray easily off the beaten path. Buses run to most places you might want to go, and the train is the handiest option for tripping along the south coast.

🚗 Car

Hiring a car gives you maximum flexibility and is comparatively inexpensive. Driving in Portugal is easy, but make sure you organise payment of the automated motorway tolls. Parking in the beach towns can be a problem in summer.

🚌 Bus

Buses run between all the major towns and many villages, making it the most comprehensive public-transport network. It's especially useful for exploring the Algarve's interior and the west coast, where the train doesn't reach.

🚆 Train

A line with slowish but regular services runs along the Algarve's south coast as far west as Lagos, making the train an excellent option for exploring the beach towns.

The Algarve Regions

West Coast Beaches (p102)
The west coast has utterly spectacular and gloriously unspoilt surf beaches and welcoming small towns.

⊙ **Top Experience**
Surfing the West Coast

⊙ *Via Algarviana*

Cabo de São Vicente

⊙ *Fortaleza de Sagres*

Silves & Around (p60)
This former Moorish stronghold with a castle, cathedral and museum, is one of the Algarve's most picturesque towns.

Sagres & Around (p90)
On a promontory at the end of Portugal, Sagres is a laid-back surf town offering great coastal scenery and maritime history.

⊙ **Top Experiences**
Fortaleza de Sagres
Cabo de São Vicente

Lagos & Around (p78)
Much more than a party town, postcard perfect Lagos offers top beaches, a handsome historic centre and excellent restaurants.

⊙ **Top Experience**
On the Water

Monchique & Around (p70)
An appealing hill town, Monchique straddles the long-distance Via Algarviana and has some great day hikes and a lovely spa village.

⊙ Top Experience
Via Algarviana

Tavira & Around (p38)
Set around a river, this pretty town is eminently strollable. Explore unspoilt island beaches and the gorgeous village of Cacela Velha.

⊙ Top Experience
Cacela Velha

⊙ Cacela Velha

Parque
Faro ⊙ Natural da
Cathedral Ria Formosa

Faro & Around (p22)
The region's capital has a charming waterside old town, excellent boat trips and a lively restaurant and bar scene.

⊙ Top Experiences
Faro's Cathedral

Parque Natural da Ria Formosa

Loulé & Around (p50)
With an extensive historic quarter, Loulé is an appealing base for exploration of the southern coastline and the Serra do Caldeirão.

Explore
the Algarve

Tavira (p38)
PEETER VIISIMAA/GETTY IMAGES ©

Explore

Faro & Around

The capital of the Algarve is used as merely a transit point by many tourists, but is actually a lovely little town with a charming old quarter and seductive waterside location. There's a good selection of intriguing sights and a fine choice of decent restaurants and bars. As well as being a great introduction to the region, it also makes a tempting urban base to explore it.

Region in a Day

☀ Begin your day with coffee and a pastry at the **Mercado Municipal** (p37), the modern market that's great for people-watching and browsing fresh produce. From here, you're on the right side of town to visit the **Jewish Heritage Centre** (p32), then the **Nossa Senhora do Carmo** (p31) church. If the sight of all those bones hasn't spoiled your appetite, head to nearby **Chefe Branco** (p34) for a delicious, no-frills Portuguese lunch.

☀ After lunch, stroll to the old town to explore its narrow streets. Visit the **municipal museum** (p31) for a perspective on Faro's interesting history, then climb the bell tower of the **cathedral** (p24) for great views. See those intriguing waterways and sand islands? That's where you're heading next: take a late-afternoon boat trip from the nearby dock.

☽ Dine at one of the old town's tourist-oriented but delicious restaurants; **Faz Gostos** (p33) is a reliably excellent choice. Afterwards, **O Castelo** (p37), a bar with regular events, is just a few metres away. Round out the evening with a cocktail at vivacious and elegant **Columbus Bar** (p37).

For a local's day out in Olhão, see p28.

 Top Experiences

 Local Life

💜 **Best of Faro & Around**

Getting There

🚃 **Train** Connected to coastal Algarve destinations.

🚌 **Bus** Connections to towns all over the region.

Top Experiences
Faro's Sé

The picturesque centrepiece of Faro's old town, the *sé* (cathedral) was completed in 1251, but heavily damaged in the 1755 earthquake. Standing on the historic centre's major plaza, the blocky, castlelike structure occupies what was probably the site of a Roman temple, a Visigothic cathedral and then a Moorish mosque. Only the tower gate and several chapels remain of the original Romanesque-Gothic exterior – the rest was added after the earthquake's destruction.

◉ Map p30, C4

☎ 289 823 018

www.paroquiasedefaro.org

Largo da Sé

adult/child €3/free

🕙 10am-6.30pm Mon-Fri, to 1pm Sat Jun-Aug, 10am-5pm Mon-Fri, to 1pm Sat Sep-May

Don't Miss

Bell Tower

The cathedral's bell tower offers lovely views over old Faro and beyond to the marina and bay, and the estuary and islands of the Parque Natural da Ria Formosa. You needn't fear for the thigh muscles: it's only 68 steps to the top, and there's a rest stop halfway. Apart from the orange trees, landmarks on the square below include the 18th-century Paço Episcopal; it's the successor to the previous bishops' dwelling trashed by British troops in 1596.

Church

The church's interior clearly shows the variety of architectural styles that have been applied here: vaulted Gothic chapels stand to either side of the altar and Renaissance arches divide the naves. Most of the rest is baroque, with some elaborate altarpieces in the side chapels, and a striking German-built 18th-century organ.

Museu Capitular

The cathedral museum houses an assortment of chalices and monstrances, as well as priestly vestments. There are some fine painted wooden statues that once had pride of place in altarpieces, but were superseded. More alarming is the reliquary collection, housing physical remains of various saints, including both forearms of St Boniface.

Garden

Formerly the cathedral cemetery, the garden is now notable for two small chapels. One, dating from the 17th century, is dedicated to the archangel São Miguel (St Michael). The other is a small, rather down-at-heel 18th-century shrine built of bones: this type of construction was popular at the time and was designed as a reminder of the transitory nature of our earthly life.

☑ Top Tips

▶ There's a telescope atop the bell tower, but ensure you have a €0.50 coin if you want to use it.

▶ After visiting the cathedral, make sure you pop into the curious antique tile shop on Rua da Porta Nova just across the square.

✕ Take a Break

There are several bars and restaurants in the old town for a bit of sustenance after visiting the cathedral. For a light meal or a drink with views, O Castelo (p37) is a good bet. With a pretty terrace in the heart of the old town, Vila Adentro (p35) offers some modern takes on classic Algarve dishes.

Top Experiences
Parque Natural da Ria Formosa

The eastern Algarve coast between Faro and Tavira consists of a series of offshore islands backed
by estuaries. It's a complex, fascinating landscape
offering glorious ocean beaches on the seaward
side and, on the land side, a wetland environment that's an important habitat for birds and
shellfish. Boat services from several of the towns
along this stretch head over to the islands; kayaking, nature-watching trips and simply exploring
on foot are other great ways to interact with this
unusual protected area.

⊙ Map p30, D1

www.icnf.pt

Don't Miss

Praia do Barril

On long Ilha de Tavira, this is a most character-ful beach experience. From the village of Pedras del Rei, cross a narrow bridge to the island, then walk 1.5km or take the little train (€2.40 return). At the other end you'll find a glorious beach and the remnants of an old fishing settlement, with a bar-restaurant and a cemetery of anchors from the former tuna fleet.

Ilha da Armona

This large island offers some fairly deserted stretches of sand at its eastern end, and a more sociable family-oriented scene at its western end, where there's a campsite and a village, the residents of which make their living harvesting shellfish in the estuary. You can reach the island by boat from Faro, Fuzeta or Olhão, or even wade across in places at low tide.

Kayaking

With calm waterways, offshore beaches and hidden corners, the Rio Formosa park is the ideal place to explore by kayak. Several operators, including **Lands** (☑ 289 817 466; www.lands.pt; Clube Naval, Faro Marina), offer hire and guided trips. It's the best way of getting to know the region.

Birdwatching

These tidal wetland habitats support a great variety of bird life, including many seabirds and waders, from flamingos to the emblem of the park, the purple gallinule. A great number of migratory species also stop over here in spring and autumn. Several companies run dedicated birdwatching boat tours; kayaking is another good way to spot avian life.

☑ Top Tips

▶ Be cautious around the ends of the islands, where the estuary meets the sea, as there can be strong currents.

▶ One or more of the park's islands are accessible by regular boat services from Faro, Olhão, Fuzeta and Tavira, among others.

▶ Boat tours from Faro (p31) or Tavira (p45) are a great way to get a feel for the park's geography and ecosystems.

✕ Take a Break

Most of the islands have some eating and drinking options, but little Fuzeta, a gateway to the Ilha da Armona, has a great alfresco scene. By the fish-market building, two adjacent places grill up the fresh catch at no-frills outdoor tables: **Casa A. Corvo** (☑ 914 130 029; Avenida 1º de Maio; mains €6-12; ⊙ 8am-5pm) and **Cafe dos Mestres** (☑ 910 935 089; www. facebook.com/cafedos mestres; Rua 1º de Maio 29; mains €6-13; ⊙ 8am-5pm Mon-Sat).

Local Life
Olhão: a Fishing Town

While hardly unknown to tourists, the port of Olhão, 10km east of Faro, offers the chance to explore some of the more traditional aspects of Algarvian life. With its notable market buildings, fishing heritage and down-to-earth vibe, it offers an appealingly keep-it-real contrast to some of the coast's glitzier resorts.

❶ Waterside Markets
By the water in the centre of Olhão, these two noble centenarian red-brick **buildings** (Av 5 de Outubro; ⏰7am-2pm Mon-Sat) are excellent examples of industrial architecture and house picturesque traditional fruit and fish markets that are great for nosing around. A string of simple seafood eateries and cafes make them an atmospheric spot for a bite with water views.

2 Island Beaches

Olhão is separated from the ocean by the islands and estuaries of the Parque Natural da Ria Formosa. At least three times a day, and much more frequently in summer, **boats** (www.olhao.web.pt/ horariobarcos.htm; return €3.70-4.30) run to the fabulous, extensive island beaches of Armona, Culatra and Farol from the quay just east of the markets. Zip across for a couple of hours to soak up some sun or explore the little fishing hamlets.

3 Earthy Bar

A real slice of historic Portugal, **Snack-Bar A Velha** (Av da República 16; ⊙10am-10pm Mon-Sat), a no-frills old-timers bar in the centre of town, has a nicotine-stained interior and old men playing dice. It's so authentic you can forgive the gruff welcome. Look for the tiled Schweppes sign near the facade of the parish church.

4 Local Lunch

The white, modern interior of **Tacho à Mesa** (📞289 096 734; www.facebook.com/ tachoamesaolhao; Rua Lavadouros 46; mains €8-15; ⊙lunch & dinner Tue-Sat, lunch Sun; 🛜), set back from main drag Avenida da República, plays host to some excellent traditional cooking with a cordial welcome to accompany it. With fresh produce purchased twice a day, it produces a great *cataplana* (seafood stew), superjuicy *bochechas* (pork cheeks) and other Algarvian-Alentejan delights.

5 Nature Stroll

Perfect for walking off lunch, three kilometres east of Olhão is the beautiful 60-hectare **Quinta de Marim** (www.icnf.pt; ⊙8am-8pm Mon-Fri, 10am-8pm Sat & Sun Apr-Oct, 9am-noon & 2-5pm daily Nov-Mar), where a 3km nature trail takes you through various ecosystems – dunes, saltmarshes, pine woodlands – as well as to a wildlife rescue centre and a historic water mill. The Parque Natural da Ria Formosa headquarters and interpretation centre are also here.

6 Bairro dos Pescadores

This fisher's quarter, to the northeast of the centre, is a knot of white-washed, cubical houses, often with tiled fronts and flat roofs for drying nets. Narrow lanes thread through the *bairro* (neighbourhood), and there's a definite Moorish influence, probably a legacy of long-standing trade links with North Africa.

7 Vivenda Vitória

Heading back into town, at first glance this looks like a ruined church with a bell tower, but the Vivenda Vitória is in fact the elaborate early-20th-century home of a fish-canning magnate. It's now in a ruinous state; to replace the ugly scrawls that disfigured it, the council chose to commission a major graffiti project on its walls. An unusual and striking result, but the building's future remains uncertain.

R Aboim Ascenção

⊙5

R Infante Dom Henrique

✕17 ✕12
R de Loulé
✕15

R da Atalaia

R Serpa Pinto

Igreja de Nossa
Senhora do Carmo &
Capela dos Ossos
⊙3

**Parque Natural da
Ria Formosa**

**R General Teófilo
da Trindade**

R Sotto Mayor

Merca
Munici
de Fa
(100

Largo do
Carmo

R Teófilo Braga

R Ventura Coelho
Largo do
Estação
R Francisco Barreto
19

R do Viola

R do Forno
R Gil Eanes
R da
Bargueta

R de São Pedro

R do Prior

R Conselheiro de Bivar

Largo de
São Pedro

R do Alportel

R Cruz dos Mestres

Largo das
Mouras
Velhas
23
☆

R Filipe Alistão

Largo
do Sol
Posto

Largo das
Mouras
Velhas

R Batista Lopes

R Lethes

R da Mota

R Dr Justino Cuma

Largo
de Ab

2
☐
**Train
Station**

14

R José Estêvão

Pç Ferreira
de Almeida

R Vasco da Gama

R de Portugal

22
☐

Av da República

R 1 de Maio

Largo do
Bispo

13

Museu
Regional do
Algarve

Natura
Algarve ⊙4

Parque Natural
da Ria Formosa

Praça Dom
Francisco
Gomes

R Dr F Gomes

R de Santo António

⊙
10

R do
da Cr

Marina

20
☐

✕16
R Rebelo da Silva

R Brites
Almeida

R Castilho

Jardim
Manuel
Bívar

R Alexandre
Herculano

Praça
Alexandre
Herculano

Formosamar ⊙1

R da Misericórdia

R do Albergue

R Teresa Ramalho Ortigã

R do Bocage

R Cáçadores-4

R Comandante Francisco Manuel

7 ⊙ ❶
Arco
da Vila

R Rasquinho

R de São Francisco

CIDADE VELHA

Sé
⊙

Praça Dom
Afonso III

18 ☐
11 ☐

R do Trem

R do Castelo

2
Museu
Municipal

Largo
da Sé

8 ☐
Galeria
Trem

Largo do
Castelo

21
☆

❶

Animaris ⊙9

Largo de
São Francisco

R Nova do Castelo

For reviews see

⊙	Top Experiences	p24
⊙	Experiences	p31
✕	Eating	p33
☐	Drinking	p37
☆	Entertainment	p37

Ⓝ
0 ——————— 200 m
0 ——————— 0.1 miles

↓ Ilha da Barreta;
Ilha da Culatra

Experiences

Formosamar

BOAT TOUR

1 Map p30, B4

This recommended outfit, and its stablemate Lands (p27) genuinely embrace and promote environmentally responsible tourism. Among the excellent tours it provides are two-hour birdwatching trips around the Parque Natural da Ria Formosa (€30), dolphin-watching (€45), cycling tours (€25), and walking tours inland from Faro. Its two-hour small-boat trips penetrate some of the narrower channels in the lagoon (€25). (✆918 720 002; www.formosamar.com; Clube Naval, Faro Marina)

Museu Municipal

MUSEUM

2 Map p30, C5

Faro's domed and splendid 16th-century Renaissance **Convento de Nossa Senhora da Assunção**, in what was once the Jewish quarter, houses the Museu Municipal. Highlights include the 3rd-century *Mosaic of the Ocean*, found in 1976; 9th- to 13th-century domestic Islamic artefacts; and works by a notable Faro painter, Carlos Filipe Porfírio, depicting local legends. Informative pamphlets in English detail key exhibits, including the interesting *Paths of the Roman Algarve*. The museum has regular fado performances. (✆289 897 400; Praça Dom Afonso III 14; adult/student €2/1; ⊙10am-7pm Tue-Fri, 11.30am-6pm Sat & Sun Jun-Sep, 10am-6pm Tue-Fri, 10.30am-5pm Sat & Sun Oct-May)

Igreja de Nossa Senhora do Carmo & Capela dos Ossos

CHURCH

3 Map p30, C1

This twin-towered baroque church was completed in 1719 under João V. The spectacular facade was completed after the 1755 earthquake. Brazilian gold paid for it, and the interior is gilded to the extreme. The numerous cherubs seem comparatively serious and sober, no doubt contemplating the ghoulish attraction behind the church: the 19th-century Capela dos Ossos, built from the bones and skulls of over 1000 monks as a blackly reverent reminder of earthly impermanence. It's quite a sight. (Largo do Carmo; chapel €2; ⊙9am-1pm & 3-5pm or 6pm Mon-Fri, 9am-1pm Sat, Mass 9am Sun)

Natura Algarve

BOAT TOUR

4 Map p30, B3

This eco-responsible operator offers a range of mainly boat-related activities, from all-day tours exploring the Ria Formosa (5½ hours, €52 excluding lunch) to two-hour dolphin trips (€45), 2½-hour birdwatching trips (€35) or the popular 'Natura' trip – a 2½-hour interpretative tour with explanations about history, traditions and local economy. You explore the canals as well as Ilha da Culatra. (✆918 056 674; www.natura-algarve.com; Av da República)

Milreu Ruins

RUIN

5 Map p30, C1

Set in beautiful countryside a kilometre or so out of Estói, north of Faro, these are the ruins of a Roman villa so large and grand it was originally thought to have been a town. The villa, inhabited from the 1st century AD, has the characteristic peristyle form, with a gallery of columns around a courtyard. The highlight is the temple; its fish mosaics and former central pool suggest it was devoted to a water cult. (admission €2; 9.30am-1pm & 2-6.30pm Tue-Sun May-Sep, 9am-1pm & 2-5.30pm Tue-Sun Oct-Apr)

Faro Jewish Heritage Centre

CEMETERY

6 Map p30, D1

The last vestiges of the first post-Inquisition Jewish presence in Portugal are found at the extraordinary Jewish cemetery, which has 76 beautiful marble gravestones. The small site also has a tiny museum and re-created synagogue (complete with a reconstructed wedding). Knowledgable caretaker António starts you off with a long-winded DVD, then gives a detailed, interesting tour. You'll find it tucked behind the football stadium – look for the cypresses – a kilometre from the centre; you can get close on local bus 3. (925 071 509; www.cilisboa. org/faro; Estrada da Penha; tour €3; 9am-1pm & 2-4.30pm Mon-Fri)

Arco da Vila

LANDMARK

7 Map p30, C4

Enter the Cidade Velha (Old Town) through the neoclassical Arco da Vila, built by order of Bishop Francisco Gomes (Faro's answer to the Marquês de Pombal), who oversaw the city's reconstruction after the 1755 earthquake. The top of the street opens onto the orange-tree-lined Largo da Sé, with the *câmara municipal* (town hall) on the left, the Paço Episcopal (Bishop's Palace) on the right and the ancient *sé* (cathedral) in front of you.

Galeria Trem

GALLERY

8 Map p30, C5

This attractively converted building houses temporary exhibitions by known local and international artists: painters, photographers, installation artists and sculptors. It's worth popping by to see what's on. (Rua do Trem; admission free; 11.30am-6pm Tue-Sat Jun-Sep, 10.30am-5pm Tue-Sat Oct-May)

☑ Top Tip

On the Water

Taking a boat tour is a great way to get to know the estuaries and islands. We recommend picking a late-afternoon departure for the quality of the light and the increased birdwatching opportunities.

Milreu Ruins

Animaris
BOAT TOUR

 9   Map p30, B5

Runs trips to Ilha da Barreta (Ilha Deserta). Boats (€10 to €15 return) leave from southeast of the marina, in front of the walls of Cidade Velha. There's also a ticket office by the marina. You can include a nature circuit or charter a private speedboat to the island (€50 one way). (☏ 917 811 856, 918 779 155; www.animaris.pt)

Museu Regional do Algarve
MUSEUM

10   Map p30, D3

Elements of old peasant life – such as a small fishing boat and a wooden

water cart (used until the owner's death in 1974) – are on display, along with ceramics, fabrics and dioramas of typical interiors. Labelling is scarce; basic written information is available in English and other languages. (☏ 289 827 610; Praça da Liberdade; adult/concession €1.50/1; ⏱ 10am-1.30pm & 2.30-6pm Mon-Fri)

Eating

Faz Gostos
PORTUGUESE, FRENCH €€

11   Map p30, C5

Elegantly housed in the old town, this restaurant offers high-class French-influenced Portuguese cuisine in a spacious, comfortably handsome dining area. There's plenty of game,

> ## Understand
> ### A Short History of Faro
>
> After the Phoenicians and Carthaginians, Faro boomed as the Roman port Ossonoba. During the Moorish occupation it became the cultured capital of an 11th-century principality. It was taken by Afonso III in 1249, making it the last major Portuguese town to be recaptured from the Moors.
>
> Faro had a brief golden age that came to a halt in 1597, during Spanish rule. Troops under the earl of Essex, en route to England from Spain, plundered the city and carried off hundreds of priceless theological works from the bishop's palace; the books are now part of the Bodleian Library in Oxford.
>
> Battered Faro was rebuilt only to be shattered by an earthquake in 1722 and then damaged again in 1755. Much of what you see today was built postquake, although, compared to the rest of southern Portugal, the historic centre largely survived. In 1834 Faro became the Algarve's capital.

fish and meat on offer with rich and seductive sauces, and a few set menus are available. (☑289 878 422; www.fazgostos.com; Rua do Castelo 13; mains €14-20; ☺lunch & dinner Mon-Fri, dinner Sat; ☎)

Chefe Branco   PORTUGUESE €

 Map p30, A1

A fabulous local spot with a cosy feel and appealing streetside seating. The delightful staff serve honest, homestyle fare including rabbit, goat and seafood dishes. The half portions are the biggest this side of the Rio Tejo. Serves excellent Algarvian desserts, too. (Rua de Loulé 9; mains €6-12; ☺noon-11pm)

Gengibre e Canela   VEGETARIAN €

 Map p30, D3

Give the taste buds a break from meat and fish dishes and veg out (literally) at this Zen-like vegetarian restaurant.

The buffet changes daily; there may be vegetable lasagne, vegetarian *feijoada* (bean casserole) and tofu dishes. (☑289 882 424; Travessa da Mota 10; buffet €7.50; ☺noon-3pm Mon-Sat; ☎✈)

Maktostas   CAFE €

 Map p30, C2

This worthwhile spot has a downbeat retro interior where students and Faro bohemians of all ages gather for the delicious and enormous open toasties, daily specials or a few beers. The tree-shaded terrace out the front, looking over a peaceful square, is even better. Understated and excellent. (Rua do Alportel 29; dishes €4-9; ☺8am-2am; ☎)

Restaurante O Murta   SEAFOOD €

 Map p30, A1

This simple place has been here for decades so it must be doing something right. It grills up quality meat and fish, and prepares excellent seafood dishes such as *açorda de marisco* (seafood stew in a bread bowl) and its signature *bacalhau* (salt-cod) dish, prepared with piri-piri and chilli. (www.facebook.com/OMurta; Rua Infante Dom Henrique 136; mains €6-10; ☉lunch & dinner Mon-Sat)

Gardy
PATISSERIE €

 16 Map p30, D3

The place to head for your patisserie fix and *the* place to be seen. Has a wide variety of homemade specialities. (☏289 824 062; Rua de Santo António 16; pastries €0.50-4; ☉8.30am-7.30pm Mon-Sat; 🛜)

Santo António Atelier de Comida
PORTUGUESE €€

17 Map p30, A1

Modern in design rather than cuisine, this place has a confusing entrance and an open kitchen. Trendy seating abounds, but there are few fripperies on the lengthy menu, which excels with juicy cuts of pork and delicious barbecued whole fish. Quality tastes are sometimes paired with curious presentation, but once it's in your mouth, who minds? (☏289 802 148; www.jfsantoantonio.pt; Praça Largo Camões 23; mains €6-15; ☉lunch & dinner; 🛜)

Vila Adentro
PORTUGUESE €€

 18 Map p30, C5

With streetside tables in old Faro and a handsome dining area decorated with bright furniture and lovely tiled panels, this conversion of a historic building has a lot going for it. Service is multilingual and well meaning, and the kitchen turns out interesting and tasty flavour combinations from local traditions and further afield. (☏933 465 188; www.vilaadentro.pt; Praça Dom Afonso III 17; mains €12-18; ☉9am-midnight)

Adega Nova
PORTUGUESE €€

 19 Map p30, A2

Dishing up simply grilled fish and meat, this popular place has plenty of country charm. It has a lofty beamed ceiling, rustic cooking implements on display and long communal tables and bench seats. Service is efficient. (☏289 813 433; www.restauranteadeganova.com; Rua Francisco Barreto 24; mains €7.50-18; ☉11.30am-11pm)

Local Life
Cheap Eats

A favourite spot among locals, **Pastelaria Coelho** (Rua Brites de Almeida 2; mains €3-7; ☉7.30am-midnight) has to be the most deceptive spot in Faro. It looks like a typical pastry- and coffee-stop from the outside, yet inside, it morphs into a restaurant, and serves up some hearty daily specials for a Portuguese song. Think everything from *xarém* (maize meal with meat or fish) to turkey stew.

Understand
Sustainable Tourism in the Algarve

‑ ‑

Concentrated Development
Much of Portugal's important tourism industry is focused on the Algarve, which went from what, in the 1960s, was still a quiet string of fishing villages, to a heavily developed coastline geared up for mass tourism. And we're not just talking foreign visitors; domestic visitors comprise a large part of the industry – numerous Portuguese people have homes in this sun-kissed region – and many expats have moved here permanently. The massive influx of visitors has led to ongoing heavy development along much of the Algarve's southern coastline. While the Algarve's tourism industry provides work – albeit seasonal – to thousands of people, concerns have been raised about the impact on the environment caused by the construction of large (mainly concrete) hotels, apartments, shops and restaurants, and the building of dozens of golf courses and major roads. Destruction of coastal areas, including cliffs and beaches, and pressure on water resources are among the important issues. And while construction has been better controlled in recent years, it is not always sensitive to its surrounds.

New Strategies
The local tourism authorities have been making a big effort to develop a more sustainable future for the Algarve and have focused their efforts on promoting special-interest activities beyond sun and sand. Through this positive initiative, the region's spectacular nature, walks and countryside have increasingly been highlighted, spreading the benefits of tourism to the inland villages.

Here, small museums give insights into local traditions and culture, marked walking routes let you explore at a less frenetic pace and with no carbon guilt, and local craftspeople sell everything from hand-painted ceramics to seriously potent moonshine.

Making a Difference
So what's the best way to enjoy the Algarve sustainably? Think carefully about the impact of your travels, and the activities you undertake, on this sensitive region; head inland and visit smaller communities and spend your money in local businesses. Sounds too worthy? Think about it as ordering another glass of that tasty local red in the village restaurant: good news for everyone involved.

Drinking

Columbus Bar
BAR

20 Map p30, C3

Definitely the place to be, this popular central place has a streetside terrace in the heart of town and an attractive brick-vaulted interior. Bar staff do a fine job mixing cocktails, and there's a pleasing range of spirits. Gets lively from around 11pm onwards. (www.barcolumbus.pt; Praça Dom Francisco Gomes 13; ⊙noon-4am; 🛜)

O Castelo
BAR

21 Map p30, C5

Smart O Castelo is all things to all people: a bar, restaurant, nightclub and performance space. Start your day here with a coffee, grab a light meal for lunch or take in sunset over a cocktail. In summer the outside morphs into a party and performance space, and there are regular concerts. Its location, perched atop the historic walls of the old town, is superb. (www.facebook.com/OCasteloCidadeVelha; Rua do Castelo 11; ⊙10am-4am summer, 11am-4am winter; 🛜)

Bar Chessenta
BAR

22 Map p30, C3

A miracle of split-levelling has managed to fit two floors, toilets and a stage for live music into this tiny space. Right in the heart of Faro's bar zone,

the Chessenta is bohemian and simple, with a Che Guevara theme. (www.facebook.com/bar.chessenta; Rua do Prior 24; ⊙4pm-4am Mon-Thu, 9pm-4am Fri-Sun; 🛜)

Entertainment

Teatro Lethes
THEATRE

23 ⭐ Map p30, D2

This tiny and exquisite Italianate theatre hosts drama, music and dance performances. Adapted into a theatre in 1874 (from a building dating to 1603), it was once the Jesuit Colégio de Santiago Maior. Check its website or ask the tourist office for a list of what's on; you can buy tickets online. Other performances are often held in the modern Teatro Figuras. (📞289 878 908; www.actateatro.org.pt/teatrolethes; Rua Lethes)

Explore

Tavira & Around

Set on either side of the meandering Rio Gilão, Tavira is a charming place. Its characterful *centro histórico* (old town) and enticing assortment of restaurants and guesthouses make it an excellent base for exploring the eastern Algarve. Near it are some seductive bits of coast, including the lovely village of Cacela Velha and the unspoilt beaches of Ilha de Tavira.

Region in a Day

☀ Grab a coffee and pastry at classic Portuguese cafe **Pastelaria Tavirense** (p48), then set about exploring the *centro histórico*. By the *turismo* (tourist office) you'll find the **Núcleo Islâmico** (p45) museum, and close by is the impressive **Igreja da Misericórdia** (p45). Time your visit to take in the melancholic strains of a fado performance at the adjacent **Fado Com História** (p49), then stroll the upper town, ticking off the peaceful garden of the **Castelo** (p45) and the camera obscura at the **Torre da Tavira** (p46). Head over one of the bridges for lunch at **Casa Simão** (p46).

☀ From Quatro Águas, take a short boat ride across to the **Ilha de Tavira** (p45) and work off lunch pacing the sands and appreciating the estuarine ecosystem. Alternatively, take a boat tour of the area with **Passeios Ria Formosa** (p45).

☾ Amble the riverside in the evening, and take your pick of dinner restaurants, perhaps **A Barquinha** (p48) or **Aquasul** (p48). In summer there's plenty of bar action around the north side of the river. For a more tranquil cocktail, head to **Tavira Lounge** (p48) just outside the old town.

For a local's day out along the Guadiana river, see p42.

👁 Top Experiences

Cacela Velha (p40)

🔍 Local Life

Along the Guadiana (p42)

💜 Best of Tavira & Around

Beaches
Ilha de Tavira (p45)

Praia do Barril (p45)

Praia de Cacela Velha (p40)

Praia Fluvial de Alcoutim (p43)

Historic Architecture
Castelo de Tavira (p45)

Castelo de Castro Marim (p43)

Castelo de Alcoutim (p42)

Dining
Casa Simão (p46)

A Fábrica do Costa (p41)

Getting There

🚆 **Train** Regular trains from Faro, with connections from Lisbon and elsewhere.

🚌 **Bus** Frequent buses from Faro and further afield.

Top Experiences
Cacela Velha

Small, enchanting and cobbled, the gorgeous village of Cacela Velha is a huddle of white-washed cottages edged with bright borders, and has a pocket-sized fort, orange and olive groves, and gardens blazing with colour. It's 14km east of Tavira, looking out over the estuary and ocean beyond, with a couple of excellent cafe-restaurants, splendid views and a meandering path down to the waterside. It's one of the Algarve's real beauty spots.

◉ Map p44, D2

14km east of Tavira off the N125

Don't Miss

Igreja de Nossa Senhora da Assunção

The centrepiece of the village, like many of the Algarve's churches, has architectural features from a range of periods. Though the church dates from the 13th century, only a Gothic side door survives from the original construction; the interior conserves some Renaissance-era arches, while most of the rest is baroque, dating from both before and after the 1755 earthquake, which caused major damage.

Fortaleza

The village's fortress occupies a position that commands the coast in both directions and is still used by the National Republican Guard, so is not open to the public. Once a Moorish castle, it suffered various periods of decay and rebuilding; what you see today dates from the late 18th century. The walkway behind the church gives a good idea of the fortress' outlook.

Fábrica

A kilometre by road from Cacela Velha, or a lovely coastal stroll, brings you to the village of Fábrica, a tiny base for fisherfolk and shellfish pickers. It's a reminder that despite Cacela's jewel-like beauty, it's still a small traditional community.

Praia de Cacela Velha

Lonely and lovely, this bow-shaped spit of sand is divided from the mainland by an estuary. It can be reached by walking a couple of kilometres west from the beach at Manta Rota, or by hiring a boat across the estuary from Fábrica. It's one of the least crowded of all the Algarve beaches; there's a low-key LGBTIQ scene here in summer.

☑ Top Tips

▶ Cacela gets busy: a visit early in the morning or late in the afternoon is recommended for serenity and the best light.

▶ Though it can feel like a museum village, these are people's homes, so be sensitive when snapping photos of those lovely white houses.

✕ Take a Break

For an alfresco beer in the heart of the village, or simple local fare, **Casa da Igreja** (Largo da Igreja; mains €5-15; ⊙9am-10pm) is a very traditional *tasca* (tavern) near the church.

In Fábrica, the superb position of **A Fábrica do Costa** (☑281 951 467; Sítio da Fábrica, Cacela Velha; mains €11-19; ⊙9.30am-2am) makes it the romantic choice.

Local Life
Along the Guadiana

Forming the border with Spain, the Rio Guadiana has plenty to offer along its banks, with castles, nature reserves, a riverside beach and a seaside town to explore. This drive makes a great day trip from Tavira and takes in some of the Algarve's lesser-visited corners.

❶ Road to the Hills

It's a picturesque drive from Tavira north along the N397, which rises into the Algarve's hilly interior. The sweet village of Cachopo is a typical highland settlement, with steep, somnolent streets.

❷ Alcoutim's Castle

The flower-ringed, 14th-century **castelo** (admission €2.50; ⏰9.30am-7pm Apr-Sep, 8.30am-4.30pm Oct-Mar) at Alcoutim has

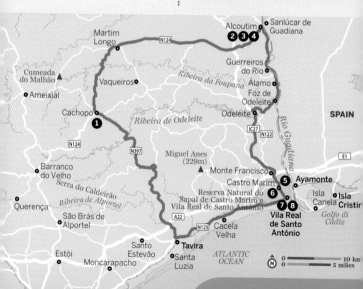

sweeping views. Inside the grounds is an excellent archaeological museum, displaying ruined medieval castle walls and other artefacts, and an exhibition on Islamic board games.

❸ An Unusual Beach

Forget the Algarve's 150-plus ocean beaches, Alcoutim's cute little riverside **Praia Fluvial** is where it's at. Though languidly set on a bend in a narrow tributary of the Guadiana, don't you dare say backwater: it's equipped with sand, cafe, palm-leaf umbrellas and even a lifeguard! The setting is lovely, though it gets baking hot in summer.

❹ Hearty Lunch

Alcoutim has a handful of good places to eat, but **O Camané** (Rua 1 de Maio; mains €8-14; ◷lunch & dinner Wed-Mon), near the river in the heart of town, makes a top lunch stop. It's a popular spot bursting with a range of Algarvian and Alentejan dishes, including *porco preto* (Iberian pig) and *açorda* (bread soup). There's always a good selection of daily specials.

❺ Birdwatchers' Wetland

The off-the-beaten-track **Reserva Natural do Sapal de Castro Marim** (☎281 510 680; ◷9am-12.30pm & 2-5.30pm Mon-Fri) is Portugal's oldest, covering marshland and salt pans bordering the Rio Guadiana. Important winter visitors include greater flamingos, spoonbills and Caspian terns; in spring it's busy with white storks.

The park headquarters is 2km east of the N122 from a signposted turn-off 1.5km north of Castro Marim. Here there's a 500m trail with faded interpretative signboards.

❻ Mighty Fortress

The huge **castle** (admission €1.10; ◷9am-7pm Apr-Oct, to 5pm Nov-Mar) complex dominating the small town of Castro Marim has an intriguing borderland history. Much of the area was destroyed in the 1755 earthquake, but the ruins of the main fort are still amazing. Inside the walls is a 14th-century church, the Igreja de Santiago, where Prince Henry the Navigator is said to have prayed.

❼ Border Town

Staring across at Ayamonte in Spain over the Rio Guadiana, Vila Real de Santo António has become far quieter since the international ferry (still active) was superseded by a motorway bridge. Designed on a grid pattern by the Marquês de Pombal after the town was destroyed by floods, the small pedestrian centre is architecturally impressive; it's very pleasant to stroll around here and the nearby waterfront.

❽ Sundowner with a View

On the water side of the waterfront road in Vila Real, the **Associação Naval do Guadiana** (Av da República; mains €9-17; ◷11.45am-3pm & 6.30-10.30pm; 🛜) has the best views in town. It does good seafood in the restaurant, but for an even better vista, head upstairs to the bar.

A
12

B

C
8

D

0 200
0 .... 0.1 miles

N

R Prof Egas Moniz

R da Porta Nova

R Fumeiros Detrás
R Fumeiros
de Diante

Largo do
Carmo

R dos Limpinhos

R de Sant'Ana

Largo de
Santana

Cç de Sant'Ana

Largo de
São Brás

Rua Chefe António Afonso

Rio Séqua

R João Vaz Corte Real

R Borda d'Água da Asséca

Praça
Dr António
Padinha

R Dr Augusto
Silva Carvalho

R Álvares Botelho

R da Oliveira

R do Salto

Cacel
Velh

15
17
9

11

R Dr A Cabreira

Tv Jaques
Pessoa

R Almirante Cândido dos Reis

R Dr Jaques Pessoa

18

Largo do
Trem

R Poeta Emiliano da Costa

R José Joaquim Jara

R Comandante
Henrique Brit

Ponte Romana
(pedestrian only)

R dos Pelames

R Gonçalo
Velho

16

Praça da
República

Ponte das
Forças Armadas

Tv da Caracolinha

R Borda d'Água de Aguia

Rio Gilão

R dos Bombeiros Municipais

R Detraz dos Muros

Cç Dona Ana

Palácio da
Galeria

Cç da
Galeria

6
20
4

3

Núcleo
Islâmico

R do Cais

Cç da Galeria

Largo

19

R Dr José Pires Padinha

Mercado da
Ribeira

1

7

Abu-Otmane

Igreja da
Misericórdia

P

5

Torre da
Tavira

Castelo

14

21

R Dr Parreira

13

Largo da
Porta do
Postigo

R D Paio Peres Correia

R da Liberdade

R Dr Marcelino Franco

Tv de Garção

R 31 de Janeiro

R António Viegas

R Dr Augusto
Carlos Palma

R Tenente Couto

R Guilherme Gomes Fernandes

R Montalvão

R Dr Silvestre Falcão

P

R 1º de Maio

R dos Machados

R Dr Miguel Bombarda

Av Dr Teixeira de Azevêdo

Praça Zacarias
Guerreiro

10

P

R 25 de Abril

R do Poeta
Isidoro Pires

Campo dos
Mártires
da Pátria

P

Santa Luzia
(2.5km)

2

Santa Luzia
(250m)

Experiences

Ilha de Tavira ISLAND, BEACH

1 Map p44, D3

Sandy islands (part of the Parque Natural da Ria Formosa) stretch along the Algarve's east coast; this is one of the finest. The huge beach at the eastern end, opposite Tavira, has water sports, camping ground and cafe-restaurants. The island, reached by a ferry from Quatro Águas, 2km from Tavira, usually feels wonderfully remote and empty, but during July and August it's busy.

Praia do Barril BEACH

2 Map p44, B5

On long Ilha de Tavira, this is a most characterful beach experience. From the village of Pedras d'el Rei, cross a narrow bridge to the island, then walk 1.5km, or take the little train, to find a glorious beach and the remnants of an old fishing settlement, with a bar-restaurant and a cemetery of anchors from the former tuna-fishing fleet. (www.barrilisland.com; ☉train 8.30am-10pm Jun-Sep, 9am-5pm Oct-May)

Núcleo Islâmico MUSEUM

3 Map p44, B3

This small, modern museum exhibits impressive Islamic pieces discovered in various excavations around the old town. There's an introductory video downstairs; one of the most important finds on display upstairs is the *Tavira Vase,* an alaborate ceramic work with figures and animals around the rim. Multilingual handouts are available at reception. (Praça da República 5; adult/child €2/1, joint admission with Palácio da Galeria €3/1.50; ☉10am-12.30pm & 3-6pm mid-Jun–mid-Sep, 10am-4.30pm Tue-Sat mid-Sep–mid-Jun)

Igreja da Misericórdia CHURCH

4 Map p44, B3

Built in the 1540s, this church is the Algarve's most important Renaissance monument, with a magnificent carved, arched doorway. Inside, the restrained Renaissance arches contrast with the cherub-heavy baroque altar; tiled panels depict the works of Mercy. Behind is a museum with a rather effeminate St John, salvers, chalices, and a hall with an interesting 18th-century apple-wood ceiling and elegant furniture. (Rua da Galeria; admission free; ☉9am-1pm & 2-6pm Mon-Sat)

Passeios Ria Formosa BOAT TOUR

Offers various boat trips in the Ria Formosa protected area, with departures from **Santa Luzia** (sales office Avenida Eng Duarte Pacheco) and **Cabanas** (Avenida 28 de Maio) near Tavira, as well as from **Olhão** (Avenida 5 de Outubro) and **Fuzeta** (Avenida Dr César Oliveira). Choices range from hour-long cruises (€12.50) to all-day explorations of the offshore islands and ecosystems (€50). (☎962 156 922; www.passeios-ria-formosa.com)

Castelo CASTLE

5 Map p44, B4

Tavira's ruined castle rises high and mighty above the town. Possibly dating back to Neolithic times, rebuilt by

Local Life
Santa Luzia

The fishing village of Santa Luzia is effectively a district of Tavira these days, and is a recommended place to wander to get a feel for typical Algarve life. Overlooking the channel that separates the mainland from the Ilha de Tavira, it's famous for *polvo* (octopus), which you can try in restaurants along the main road. Have a nose around the fishers storage huts, where you'll see them mending nets. Boat trips also leave from the waterfront here.

Phoenicians and later taken over by the Moors, most of what now stands is a 17th-century reconstruction. The interior holds a very pleasant botanic garden, and the octagonal tower offers fine views over Tavira. Note that the ramparts and steps are without railing. (Largo Abu-Otmane; admission free; ⊙8am-5pm Mon-Fri, 9am-7pm Sat & Sun, to 5pm winter)

Palácio da Galeria
MUSEUM

6 Map p44, B3

This elegant palace has a permanent collection on the town of Tavira supplemented by changing seasonal exhibitions. (☑281 320 540; Calçada da Galeria; adult/child €2/1; ⊙10am-12.30pm & 3-6pm Tue-Sat Apr-Oct, 10am-4.30pm Nov-Mar)

Torre da Tavira
VIEWPOINT

7 Map p44, B3

The Torre da Tavira, which was formerly the town's water tower (100m), now houses a camera obscura. A simple but ingenious object, the camera obscura reveals a 360-degree panoramic view of Tavira, its monuments and local events, in real time – all while you are stationary. (www.torredetavira.com; Calçada da Galeria 12; adult/child €4/2; ⊙10am-5pm Mon-Fri, to 1pm Sat Jul-Sep, 10am-5pm Mon-Fri Feb-Jun, to 4pm Oct-Jan)

Kitesurf Eolis
KITESURFING

8 Map p44, C1

Highly professional outfit based at Cabanas de Tavira, around 6km east of Tavira, offering kitesurfing classes and a range of other water sports. (☑962 337 285; www.kitsurfeolis.com; Ria Formosa 38, Centro Comercial, Shop 33, Cabanas de Tavira)

Eating

Casa Simão
PORTUGUESE €

9 Map p44, B2

We'll be upfront: this old-style, barn-like eatery has harsh lighting and zero romance, but that's because the delightful family-owners concentrate on down-to-earth fare – they whip up great-value meals such as *javali estufado* (wild boar stew) and grills. Go for the daily specials. (João Vaz Corte Real 10; mains €6-11; ⊙noon-3pm & 7-10pm Mon-Sat)

Restaurante Avenida
PORTUGUESE €€

10 Map p44, B5

This very authentic, well-maintained Portuguese place with gold-and-blue tablecloths has an air of the 1960s, efficiency with a capital 'E', and a loyal

Understand

Seafood Dishes of the Algarve

Portugal's maritime history has meant that fishing has always been a big part of life; the Algarve is heaven for any lover of the fruits of the sea, with lots of fresh produce prepared in various ways.

There's a huge range of fish, often deliciously served simply grilled over charcoal. Common species include *robalo* (sea bass), *dourada* (gilthead bream), *corvina* (meagre) and the very typical *sardinha* (sardine), along with its mackerel cousins *sarda* and *carapau*. Many Portuguese would consider *sardinhas assadas* (grilled sardines) as their national dish, and it's an inexpensive and tasty treat. Fish is often listed on menus as a price per kilo; think 200g to 400g for a decent-sized whole fish.

Other sea creatures commonly devoured include *lula* (squid), *polvo* (octopus) and *choco* (cuttlefish). The *camarão* (prawn) is a staple, and you'll see other crustaceans such as the *sapateira* (literally a 'shoe-maker', but in this case the brown crab).

Bivalves, numerous in the coastal estuaries of the eastern Algarve, also enliven menus. *Amêijoas* (clams), *ostras* (oysters), *berbigões* (cockles), *mexilhões* (mussels) and *lingueirões* (razor clams) make their way into lots of dishes. *Perceves* (goose barnacles), looking like a chewed fingernail on a rubber tube, are a challenge at first sight but a worthwhile delicacy.

The Algarve's signature dish is the *cataplana*, named after the flying-saucer-like steel or copper pan it is cooked in. It's often lazily labelled the 'Portuguese paella', but isn't actually very similar, and doesn't usually contain rice. The pan's tight seal produces delicious combinations of, typically, seafood and fish steamed in a wine, garlic and tomato sauce. Restaurants usually only serve it for two or more customers.

Other common dishes include seafood rices, typically served fairly liquid. *Arroz de marisco* is the standard version, but look out for *arroz de lingueirão*, with razor clams. *Açorda* is a thick soupy mixture of bread, garlic, eggs and fish (*de peixe*) or seafood (*de marisco*), while *caldeirada* is a rich broth of fish and shellfish. The unusual but typical *xarém* is an Algarvian dish of corn porridge usually containing clams.

clientele. Good homestyle dishes include the seafood risotto and grilled tuna. Service is exceptional and the quality is solid. (☑281 321 113; Av Dr Teixeira de Azevêdo 6; mains €8-12; ☺lunch & dinner Wed-Mon; 🛜)

Aquasul INTERNATIONAL €€

 11 Map p44, C2

You won't hear too much Portuguese spoken here, given this restaurant's popularity among foreigners and expats, but this Dutch-run place serves up some tasty international dishes in a cosy, mosaic-filled environment. The owners make an effort to source sustainably from the market. (☑281 325 166; www.facebook.com/restaquasul; Rua Dr Augusto Silva Carvalho 13; mains €11-19; ☺6.30-10pm Tue-Sat; 🛜🍴)

Restaurante O Ciclista PORTUGUESE €€

12 Map p44, A1

Just beyond the N125 bridge, this isolated barnlike spot stands out on its own, but pulls the local crowds. Seafood here is fresh, grilled and served by the kilo, and meat dishes are also well prepared. Good value and generous in quantity. (☑281 325 246; www.restauranteociclista.pt; Rua João Vaz Corte Real; mains €8-13, fish per kg €25-55; ☺lunch Mon, lunch & dinner Tue-Sun; 🛜🍴)

A Barquinha PORTUGUESE €€

13 Map p44, D4

One of the better choices on this restaurant-heavy riverside street, this cluttered, narrow eatery is hospitable and cosy. A Barquinha does simple things well, with tasty salads and fresh grilled local fish the way to go. You may have to knock at the door to be admitted. (Rua Dr José Pires Padinha 142; mains €7-13; ☺noon-3pm & 7-10.30pm Thu-Tue)

Pastelaria Tavirense PATISSERIE €

14 Map p44, C4

Of all the *pastelarias* (pastry and cake shops), this one serves up the best pastries, plus good soups and snacks for those on a budget. (Rua Dr Marcelino Franco 17; pastries €0.50-3; ☺8am-midnight; 🛜)

Churrasqueira O Manel PORTUGUESE €

15 Map p44, C2

A reliable place to come for *frango no churrasco* (grilled chicken) with salad (it's spot on; the owner has been at the grill for decades). Takeaway also available. (☑281 323 343; Rua Dr António Cabreira 39; grilled chicken €8; ☺lunch & dinner)

Drinking

Tavira Lounge CAFE, BAR

16 Map p44, B3

By day it's a cafe-restaurant, by night a cafe-bar. Several inviting spaces ensure a long and comfortable visit. There are even distractions for the kids. (☑281 381 034; www.taviralounge.com; Rua Gonçalo Velho 16-18; ☺noon-2am Mon-Sat Jun-Sep, reduced hours Oct-May; 🛜)

Local Life

Traditional Tasca

Amid all the touristy bustle of Tavira, it's a real pleasure to drop into **Tasca do Zé André** (Map p44; B2; Rua João Vaz Corte Real 36; ☺10am-midnight Wed-Mon), a tiny, authentic place with its cordial boss and range of ageing liqueur bottles under the Portugal scarfs behind the bar. It's great for an ice-cold *imperial* (small draught beer) or a coffee, but it also puts on good-value salads, toasts and deli tapas.

Távila   BAR

 17 Map p44, C2

Overlooking a small tree-filled plaza, this low-key *pastelaria* is popular as a bar with locals. It has outdoor tables, ideal for an afternoon or evening drink. (Praça Dr António Padinha 50; ☺8am-midnight; 🛜)

Sítio Cafe   CAFE

18 Map p44, C2

This is a popular local spot for a light lunch or an evening drink, and one of the few places with any atmosphere out of season. Divided into three parts (outside, light-inside and dark-inside), it has decent house wine and does tasty toasted sandwiches. (Largo do Trem; ☺8am-midnight Mon-Sat; 🛜)

Entertainment

Fado Com História   FADO

19 ⭐ Map p44, B3

This sweet space in old Tavira gives you a decent introduction to Lisbon-style fado with a video and then a short performance. The whole thing goes for about half an hour, with shows in the morning and afternoon. It's aimed at tourists, but the quality is good. (☏968 774 613; www.facebook.com/fadocomhistoria; Rua Damião Augusto de Brito Vasconcelos 4; admission €5; ☺6 shows daily Mon-Sat)

Shopping

Casa do Artesão   HANDICRAFTS

20 🔒 Map p44, B3

This handicrafts collective in the heart of the old town makes a fine spot to shop for traditional basketware, cloth, ceramics and *aguardente* (distilled fruit spirit). (www.asta.pt; Calçada da Galeria 11; ☺10am-1pm & 2-5.30pm)

Garrafeira Soares   DRINK

21 🔒 Map p44, D4

Opposite the market building, this outlet has a good selection of Portuguese wines, ports and spirits at fair prices. (www.garrafeirasoares.pt; Rua Dr José Pires Padinha 66; ☺9am-6pm Mon-Sat)

Explore

Loulé & Around

The fast-growing inland town of Loulé is handily situated between the hills of the interior and the coast. It's a pleasant place in itself, with a charming and compact historic centre and several interesting sights in and around town. The touristy but lively resort town of Albufeira, as well as some great beaches, are just a short drive away.

Region in a Day

 First up, make your way to historic **Café Calcinha** (p58) for Loulé's best caffeine jolt, then take a stroll around the neo-Moorish **Mercado Municipal** (p59) for a taste of local life. Exploring the old town is next: pace its narrow streets, making sure to visit the **Museu Municipal** (p55) and nearby chapel of **Nossa Senhora da Conceição** (p55). Then jump in the car and head west for a memorable lunch at **Veneza** (p57), one of the Algarve's best rural restaurants.

After a hearty meal, head to the coast, where **Praia da Falésia** (p55) makes a picturesque spot to soak up some rays or walk off the calories. Relax, but make sure you leave the seaside in time to visit the fabulous tiled church of **São Lourenço de Matos** (p55) on your way back towards Loulé.

A romantic Greek dinner at **O Grego** (p58) is a pleasant way to enjoy the evening. For an after-dinner drink, you couldn't do better than **Poeta Caffe** (p58), just a short wander away through the old town.

For a local's day out in Serra do Caldeirão, see p52.

 Local Life

Serra do Caldeirão (p52)

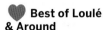 **Best of Loulé & Around**

Dining
Vila Joya (p57)

Veneza (p57)

Monte da Eira (p57)

Historic Architecture
Igreja de São Lourenço de Matos (p55)

Nossa Senhora da Conceição (p55)

Cafes
Agua Mel (p53)

Café Calcinha (p58)

Families
Aquashow (p56)

Aqualand (p57)

Albufeira Riding Centre (p56)

Getting There

 Bus Regular buses to Loulé and Albufeira from Faro and elsewhere.

Train Not convenient for Loulé or Albufeira.

Local Life
Serra do Caldeirão

North of Loulé, this is a beautiful protected area of undulating hills, cork oaks and scrubland. Hiking, birdwatching, pretty hill villages and hearty mountain cuisine are all on offer. Explorable as a day trip, the region also appeals as a place to stay, with worthwhile accommodation options. On weekends, do this itinerary in reverse, as you'll miss the toy workshop anyway.

1 Alte

One of two main towns in the Serra, Alte is a compact village boasting flower-filled streets, whitewashed buildings and several *fontes* (traditional water sources). The *fontes* were traditionally used for the mills and former wells; the largest, Fonte Grande, passes through dykes, weirs and watermills. Several *artesanatos* (handicrafts shops) are dotted around town, and the small **Pólo Museológico**

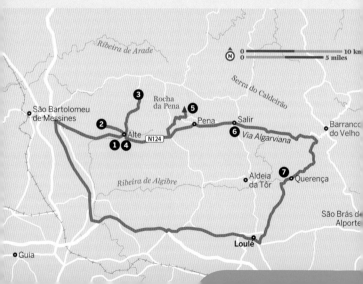

Cândido Guerreiro e Condes de Alte
museum (📞289 478 058; Rua Condes de Alte, Alte; admission free; ⊘12.30-3pm Mon-Fri) also offers tourist information.

2 Wooden Toys

The school in the little hamlet of Torre, near Alte, had fallen into disuse because there weren't enough children. There wasn't much work around either, so three local women decided to learn a craft and put the building to use. It's now the **Fábrica de Brinquedos** (Torre/Tôr; ⊘9am-1pm Mon-Fri), a workshop where they make charming wooden toys.

3 Local Food

In the tiny hill village of Sarnadas, **Rosmaninho** (📞289 478 482; r.rosman inho@sapo.pt; Sarnadas; mains €4-10; ⊘by arrangement) is a little restaurant that was founded years ago as part of a development project. It only opens if you book a day or two ahead, and it's a spot to try very authentic hill-country food, such as boar, goat or *açorda de bacalhau* (salt-cod and bread stew).

4 Coffee & Cakes

Leave room for dessert and have it with views in one of the Algarve's best cafes: charming **Agua Mel** (www.face book.com/aguamel; Largo José Cavaco Veira, Alte; pastries €1-4; ⊘9am-6pm; 🛜) back in Alte. It's an exceedingly friendly place with a lovely outlook that turns out scrumptious cakes, pies and other sweet treats. The boss is a good source of local info and the coffee is excellent.

5 Rocha da Pena

The most worthwhile short walk in the area is to climb this **limestone rock** between Alte and Salir off the N124. There's a well-signposted 4.7km circuit up the mountain. The museums in Salir, Alte and Querença usually stock a basic map-guide. Carry water and snacks, and keep an eye on fire warnings, as bushfires occur in this area.

6 Salir

Whitewashed Salir is a sleepy, appealing hill village spread over two hills below its ruined castle, which now houses the interpretative museum **Pólo Museológico de Salir** (Largo Pedro Dias, Salir; ⊘9am-1pm & 2-5pm Mon-Fri). What's left of the castle walls dates back to the 12th century; Salir also has an attractive church.

7 Querença

Though perhaps a little over-restored, this is one of the region's prettiest villages, with whitewashed buildings set around a paved square dignified by a lovely church. There are plenty of good walks hereabouts; you can grab map pamphlets in the **Pólo Museológico da Água** (Querença; admission free; ⊘9am-1pm & 2-5pm Mon-Fri), a small museum about water use that doubles as a tourist-info office. There's a cafe on the square and a pair of decent village restaurants.

R José da Costa Guerreiro

R Ramalho Ortigão

Av 25 de Abril

Largo Gago Coutinho

Av José da Costa Mealha

Av Marçal Pacheco

R José Domingos

R do Poço

R de Portugal

R Bocage

Pç da República

R Ataíde Oliveira

Mercado Municipal

R José F Guerreiro

Tv do Mercado

R Nossa Senhora de Fátima

R Miguel Bombarda

Largo Bernardo Lopes

Nossa Senhora da Conceição

R Almeida Garrett

R 5 de Outubro

Largo Barbaça

Museu Municipal

R Municipal

Largo da Matriz

Largo Dom Pedro I

R Bicas Velhas

R Martim Moniz

R José António Madeira

Largo Afonso III

R de S Paulo

R Camilo Castelo Branco

R Engenheiro Duarte Pacheco

Largo de São Francisco

R Condestável Dom Nuno Alvares Pereira

R Nossa Senhora da Piedade

R Vasco da Gama

R de Gil Vicente

Rua Gil Vicente

Praça Manuel D'Arriaga

R de Serpa Pinto

17

14

18

22

13

20

24

16

25

21

19

23

15

200 m
0.1 miles

For reviews see	
Experiences	p55
Eating	p57
Drinking	p58

Experiences

Igreja de São Lourenço de Matos
CHURCH

1 Map p54, E4

It's well worth stopping here, just off the N125 south of Loulé, to witness a marvellous feat of tilework. A baroque masterpiece, the church is wall-to-wall blue-and-white *azulejos* (painted tiles) inside, with beautiful panels depicting the life of Roman-era São Lourenço and his grisly death-by-barbecue. It was, happily, barely damaged in the 1755 earthquake. Buses between Albu- feira (40 minutes) and Loulé (15 min- utes) stop here. (Church of St Lawrence; Rua da Igreja; admission €2; ⊙10am-1pm & 3-5pm Mon-Sat)

Museu Municipal
MUSEUM

2 Map p54, D2

Housed within Loulé's restored castle, this museum contains beautifully presented fine fragments of Bronze Age and Roman ceramics (exhibitions change every few years). A glass floor exposes excavated Moorish ruins. The admission fee includes entry to a stretch of the impressively restored, square-towered castle walls and the Cozinha Tradicional Algarvia, a re- creation of a traditional Algarve kitchen, featuring a cosy hearth, archaic implements and burnished copper. (Castelo; ☎289 400 600; www.cm- loule.pt; Largo Dom Pedro I; admission €1.50; ⊙10am-6pm Tue-Fri, to 4.30pm Sat)

Nossa Senhora da Conceição
CHAPEL

3 Map p54, D2

Situated opposite Loulé's castle, and dating from the mid-17th century, the small chapel of Nossa Senhora da Conceição has a plain facade that nonchalantly hides a heavily decorated mid-18th-century single-naved interior with a magnificent gold altarpiece. During recent excavations, an Islamic door, dating from the 3rd century, was uncovered under the floor, where it now stays, protected by glass. (Rua Dom Paio Peres Correia; admission free; ⊙9.30am- 5pm Tue-Fri, to 4pm Sat)

Praia da Falésia
BEACH

4 Map p54, A3

One of the Algarve's most impressive first glimpses of beach is this long strip of sand backed by stunning cliffs in several shades of ochre. The only prob- lem is the strand gets very crowded in summer, especially when the tide is in. In low season it's all yours. It's about 10km east of Albufeira and 21km southwest of Loulé.

Museu Municipal de Arqueologia
MUSEUM

5 Map p54, A3

This museum showcases items excavat- ed from the area (such as the castle in the village of Paderne). Pieces date from the prehistoric era to the 16th century. A highlight is a beautifully complete Neolithic vase from 5000 BC. (www.

cm-albufeira.pt; Praça da República 1, Albufeira; admission €1; ⏱9.30am-5.30pm Tue-Thu & Sat, 2-10pm Fri & Sun Jul & Aug, 9.30am-5.30pm Tue-Sun Sep-Jun)

Museu de Arte Sacra   MUSEUM

 6 Map p54, A4

This tiny museum is housed in the beautifully restored 18th-century Chapel of San Sebastian. It has a stunning gold wooden altar and exhibits sacred art from surrounding churches that survived the 1775 earthquake. (☎289 585 526; Praça Miguel Bombarda, Albufeira; admission €2; ⏱10.30am-4.30pm & 8-11pm Jul & Aug, 10.30am-4.30pm Sep-Jun)

Praia da Galé   BEACH

 7 Map p54, A4

One of the best beaches in the Albufeira region, Praia da Galé, about 6km to the west of town, is long and sandy, not so crowded, and a centre for jet skiing and waterskiing. It's easily accessible by car, but there's no direct bus service to this beach or the other beaches en route.

Zoomarine   WATER PARK

 8 Map p54, A4

Zoomarine will satisfy all desires for aqua-entertainment, with huge swimming pools and slides, as well as lakes, rides and an aquarium. However, note that there are shows featuring captive dolphins and other marine mammals. Such performances have received criticism from animal-welfare groups who claim the captivity of marine life is de-bilitating and stressful for the animals, and that this is exacerbated by human interaction. Located at Guia, 8km northwest of Albufeira. (☎289 560 300; www.zoomarine.pt; N125, Km65, Guia; adult/child €29/19; ⏱10am-7.30pm Jul–mid-Sep, reduced hours Mar-Jun & mid-Sep–Oct)

Dolphins Driven   BOAT TOUR

 9 Map p54, A4

Offers two recommended excursions from Albufeira: a 2½-hour exploration of the local sea caves and dolphin-watching, or an exploration of the caves by kayak. (☎913 113 094; www.dolphins.pt; Marina de Albufeira; tours adult/child €35/20)

Aquashow   WATER PARK

 10 Map p54, A4

In Quarteira, 10km east of Albufeira, this is a huge complex with all the usual water-park attractions, plus roller coasters, sea lions, an on-site hotel and plenty more. Book online for discounted admission. (☎289 315 129; www.aquashowparkhotel.com; Quarteira; adult/child €28/19; ⏱10am-7pm Aug, to 6.30pm July, to 5.30pm Jun & Sep, to 5pm May)

Albufeira Riding Centre   HORSE RIDING

11 Map p54, A4

On the road to Vilamoura. Offers horse rides for all ages and abilities, plus hand-led rides for kids. (☎961 269 526; www.albufeirariding.webs.com; Vale Navio Complex; 1/2hr ride €25/40)

Aqualand

WATER PARK

 12   Map p54, A4

This popular water park offers lots of slides, including a huge loop-the-loop slide, as well as rapids and numerous other attractions. (📞282 320 230; www.aqualand.pt; N125, Sítio das Areias, Alcantarilha; adult/child €22.50/16.50; ⏱10am-6pm Jul & Aug, to 5pm late Jun & early Sep)

Eating

Veneza

PORTUGUESE €€

13   Map p54, A2

Eleven kilometres north of Albufeira, this spot is famed for serving what many consider to be the Algarve's finest *cataplana* (seafood stew) – here, a delicious pork and clam combination – but in truth almost all of its dishes taste so good you'll want to return. The bean and pork soup is a meal in itself; the wine cellar, partly on display, is brilliant. Make the journey. (📞289 367 129; www.restaurantevenezia.com; Estrada de Paderne 560A, Mem Moniz; mains €10-19; ⏱dinner Wed, lunch & dinner Thu-Tue; 🛜)

Monte da Eira

PORTUGUESE €€

14   Map p54, D1

On Rte 396, 5km north of Loulé in the village of Clareanes, is this smart restaurant, the stables of a converted threshing mill, now several rooms and two outdoor terraces. People come from afar to feast on dishes of *javali* (wild boar), lamb and bean casserole, and stewed rabbit. To top it off, pick from a wine list of hundreds. (📞289 438 129; www.restaurantemontedaeira.com; Clareanes; mains €12-18; ⏱lunch & dinner Sep-Jul, dinner only Aug; 🛜🅿🚶)

Vila Joya Restaurant

MODERN EUROPEAN €€€

 15   Map p54, A4

Run by Austrian expat chef Dieter Koschina, this is regarded by many as Portugal's best fine-dining restaurant. Koschina draws on a variety of culinary influences and sources the finest of Portuguese produce to create dishes of rich elegance. Excellent service rounds out a memorable experience. (📞289 591 795; www.vilajoya.com; Estrada da Galé; degustation menu €175; ⏱sittings 1-1.45pm & 7.30-8.45pm; 🛜)

O Grego

GREEK €€

16 Map p54, D4

Low-lit, romantic and reliable, this is an authentic place serving Greek specialities. There's also a pleasant patio painted in national colours. The owner turns his hand to rather delicious desserts, including a scrumptious but decidedly un-Hellenic banoffee pie. (Rua Engenheiro Duarte Pacheco 116; dishes €4-12; ⏱7-11pm Tue-Sat)

Cantina dos Sabores

VEGETARIAN €

17 Map p54, E1

In a new location, this mostly vegetarian restaurant is deservedly popular for its daily specials (around €6), juices and desserts. Generous portions are filling and enjoyable. (Rua Nossa Senhora de Fátima 1; mains €5-9; ⏱lunch & dinner Mon-Sat; 🛜🍴)

Bocage

PORTUGUESE €

18 Map p54, D2

On a quiet corner on a quiet lane just off the main drag, this likeable no-frills traditional restaurant serves up solid plates of fish and meat, and has been doing so for decades. Reliable and good. (Rua Bocage 14; mains €6-10; ⏱11am-10pm Mon-Sat)

Churrasqueira Angolana

GRILL HOUSE €

19 Map p54, A1

It ain't pretty from the outside, but you don't come here for the setting, nor for the service – it's brusque, busy and food-focused. But you'll get a decent grill here, from tuna steaks to chicken. (Rua Nossa Senhora da Piedade 63; mains €7-13; ⏱lunch & dinner Mon-Sat)

Drinking

Poeta Caffe

BAR

20 Map p54, D3

With a lovely patio terrace under the shade of trees, this friendly bar has a sweet old-town location and a great local scene. It's the best place to sip a gin and tonic on a hot evening in Loulé. (Rua Vice Almirante Cândido dos Reis 19; ⏱1pm-4am Mon-Sat; 🛜)

Taberna dos Frades

BAR

21 Map p54, C2

Decorated in comfortably rustic style, this is a rather wonderful place serving good wine by the glass, decent mixed drinks and a range of tapas. It regularly hosts live-music nights, and the atmosphere is nearly always great. (www.facebook.com/taberna.dosfrades; Rua Condestável Dom Nuno Alvares Pereira; ⏱8.30am-2am Mon-Fri, 3pm-2am Sat; 🛜)

Café Calcinha

CAFE

22 Map p54, D2

This traditional 1920s-style cafe (Loulé's oldest) has marble-topped tables inside as well as alfresco pavement tables. The statue outside depicts António Aleixo, an early-20th-

Local Life
Exploring Cork

Twelve kilometres east of Loulé, São Brás de Alportel was a hot spot in the 19th-century cork heyday. The **Cork Route** (☎918 204 977; www.algarverotas.com; short/medium/full tour €10/16/28) is a fascinating guided tour that includes a traditional cork factory as well as visiting cork stacks, learning about the industry along the way.

On the tour, but also accessible separately, the **Museu Etnográfico do Trajo Algarvio** (☎289 840 100; www.museu-sbras.com; Rua Dr José Dias Sancho 61; admission €2; �10am-1pm & 2-5pm Mon-Fri, 2-5pm Sat & Sun) is a fascinating museum of local costumes and the cork industry in a former cork magnate's mansion.

century poet and former regular of the cafe. (☎289 415 763; Praça da República 67; �8am-11pm Mon-Fri, to 4pm Sat; �)

Bar Marroquia
BAR

23 Map p54, A1

Popular with a range of Loulé folk, this bar has an Arabic theme, a pool table and a cosy interior with winter fireplace. (www.facebook.com/marroquiabar; Rua Nossa Senhora da Piedade 122; �8pm-late; �)

Shopping

Mercado Municipal
MARKET

24 Map p54, E3

This lovely restored neo-Moorish market building is a great place for a wander or to buy fresh produce. (�7am-3pm Mon-Sat)

Cerâmica O Arco
CERAMICS

25 Map p54, D2

One of a few ceramics shops in Loulé, O Arco has a bright, optimistic range of flower- and fruit-themed painted pottery. (Rua dos Almadas 4; �9am-1pm & 2-6pm Mon-Sat)

Explore

Silves & Around

Topped by a spectacular castle, Silves is one of the Algarve's prettiest towns. It's also replete with history: it was an important city in Moorish times and preserves a tightly woven medieval centre. The coast near Silves has a series of beaches with postcard-perfect rock formations – a stunning sight. The resort town of Carvoeiro retains plenty of charm and also makes a good base.

Region in a Day

☼ Head straight to the **Centro de Interpretação do Património** (Largo do Município; ⊙ 9am-1pm & 2-5pm Mon-Fri), for a knowledgable rundown on the city's history, then enter the old town proper through the impressive gateway and visit the **Museu Municipal** (p65). The highlight here is the Moorish well, complete with spiral staircase. Wander up the hill, visiting first the **cathedral** (p65), then the **castle** (p65), from where you can appreciate fine views over town.

☼ A kilometre from the castle, **Recanto dos Mouros** (p67) makes an appealing lunch stop before heading south to the coast. The pretty resort town of Carvoeiro has several beaches with striking rock formations nearby. Perhaps the most beautiful is **Praia da Marinha** (p66), reachable by road or a spectacular 5.6km cliff-top path.

☾ Watch the sunset at **Restaurant Boneca Bar** (p69) near Carvoeiro before heading back to Silves for dinner. There's a group of decent restaurants near the river; try **Marisqueira Rui** (p67) for traditional grilled fish. Head to memorable **Café Ingles** (p67) for a postdinner drink.

For a local's day in Portimão and Praia da Rocha, see p62.

 Local Life

Portimão & Praia da Rocha (p62)

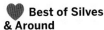 **Best of Silves & Around**

Beaches
Praia da Marinha (p66)

Praia da Rocha (p62)

Praia do Carvoeiro (p66)

Cafes
A Casa da Isabel (p62)

Café Inglês (p67)

Pastelaria Rosa (p67)

Historic Architecture
Castelo de Silves (p65)

Sé de Silves (p65)

Outdoors
Percurso dos Sete Vales Suspensos (p66)

Country Riding Centre (p66)

Getting There

🚋 **Train** The station is 2.5km south of town and trains head along the coast in both directions.

🚌 **Bus** There are some direct services, but many require a change in Lagoa or Portimão.

Local Life
Portimão & Praia da Rocha

Sixteen kilometres south-west of Silves and the Algarve's second-largest town, Portimão's history dates back to the Phoenicians, before it became the region's fishing and canning hub in the 19th century. Though that industry has since declined, it still offers plenty of maritime atmosphere. At its southern end stretches the impressive beach of Praia da Rocha.

....

❶ Wandering the Centre

Starting with a cup of tea in charming **A Casa da Isabel** (www.facebook.com/acasadaisabel; Rua Direita 61; pastries €1-5; ⏱9am-midnight Jul & Aug, to 8pm Sep-Jun; 🛜), admire some of the handsome buildings in the centre, such as the Igreja Matriz, which conserves a Gothic portal; the imposing Colégio dos Jesuítas

(Jesuit college); and the Teatro Municipal (Municipal Theatre), which houses the tourist office.

2 The Waterfront
Dotted with sculptures, the waterfront on the Rio Arade is a pleasant stroll, despite the occasionally sulphureous smell of a tidal port.

3 Largo da Barca
The old fishers' quarter is a tight web of narrow streets near the road bridge. Below, right under the arches of the bridge, is a cluster of no-frills restaurants serving charcoal-grilled sardines and mackerel. Originally catering for local fishers, these places now see crowds of visitors, but are still undeniably atmospheric.

4 Clube Naval
At the southern end of the waterfront, near the museum, the **Clube Naval do Portimão** (Restaurante do Cais; ☎282 432 325; www.facebook.com/clube.portimao; Zona Ribeirinha; mains €12-16; ☺lunch & dinner Tue-Sun; 🛜) is the spot if you like lunching with a view. The upstairs restaurant has excellent water vistas; go for the fish of the day, tuna steaks or skewers. The downstairs café is great for a waterside beverage.

5 Museu de Portimão
This cracking modern **museum** (☎282 405 230; www.museudeportimao.pt; Rua Dom Carlos I; adult/child €3/free; ☺2.30-6pm Tue, 10am-6pm Wed-Sun Sep-Jul, 7.30-11pm Tue, 3-11pm Wed-Sun Aug), housed in a 19th-century fish cannery, focuses on three areas: archaeology, underwater finds and, the most fascinating, the re-creation of the fish cannery. You can see former production lines, complete with sound effects.

6 Praia da Rocha
The ocean side of Portimão is this magnificent beach, popular with package tourists, but still a beautiful, wide stretch of sand backed by ochre red cliffs, a marina, and the petite Fortaleza da Santa Catarina, built in the 16th century to stop pirates and invaders from sailing up the Rio Arade to threaten Portimão.

7 Ocean Dining
Despite the touts outside every establishment, there's some good dining available in Praia da Rocha. **F Restaurante** (☎282 483 014; www.food-emotions.com; Av Tomás Cabreira; mains €13-20; ☺3-10.30pm Mon-Sat; 🛜) has sublime ocean views, excellent service and a quality menu of Portuguese dishes.

8 Nightlife
Tourist-oriented bars, nightclubs and a casino dot the Praia da Rocha strip, but for a more local scene, head to humble but lively **Nana's Bar** (www.facebook.com/nanasbar.praiadarocha; Rua José Bivar; ☺2pm-2am; 🛜). It's a typical Portuguese cafe, and staff pour a very decent drink.

For reviews see

⊙ Experiences   p65
✕ Eating   p67
🍷 Drinking   p69
🛍 Shopping   p69

N

0   200 m
0   0.1 miles

⊙ 6

⊙ 4

⊙ 7, 8, 9, 10

R Cândido dos Reis

R 1º de Maio

R da Cruz de Portugal

R G Mascarenhas

R do Castelo

R Diogo Manuel

R José Falcão

R do Mirante

N124

Rio Arade

Ponte
Arade

N124-1

Ponte
Velha

Castelo

⊙ 1

✕ 2

12

Sé

Lg Jerónimo
Osório

R da Sé

R da Porta de Loulé

Museu Municipal
de Arqueologia

✕ 14

R Policarpo Dias

R Elias
Garcia

R Estrada do
Monte Branco

✕ 16

R Porta da Azóia

Igreja da
Misericórdia

🍷 5

R da Misericórdia

R Joaquim A Aguiar

19

3

15

✕

R 5 de Outubro

R J Estevão

✕ 13

R Conselheiro
Vilarinho

R Francisco Pablos

R G N Mascarenhas

R Nova da Boavista

R Dom Afonso III

R Paio Pires Correia

R 25 de Abril

R Samora Barros

R João de Deus

R Miguel Bombarda

R J Menezes Barros

R Serpa Pinto

Largo da
República

R C F...

Experiences

Castelo CASTLE

1 Map p64, C2

This russet-coloured, Lego-like castle has great views over the town and countryside. Originally occupied in the Visigothic period, what you see today dates mostly from the Moorish era, though the castle was heavily restored in the 20th century. Walking the parapets and admiring the vistas is the main attraction, but you can also gaze down on the excavated ruins of the Almohad-era palace. The vaulted water cisterns, 5m deep and constructed at the end of the 12th century, now hold temporary exhibitions. (☏ 282 445 624; adult/concession/under 10yr €2.80/1.40/free, joint ticket with Museu Municipal de Arqueologia €3.90; ☉ 9am-8pm Jun-Aug, to 6.30pm Mar-May & Sep-Nov, to 5pm Dec-Feb)

Sé CATHEDRAL

2 Map p64, C2

Just below the castle is the *sé* (cathedral), built in 1189 on the site of an earlier mosque, then rebuilt after the 1249 Reconquista and subsequently restored several times following earthquake damage. In many ways, this is the Algarve's most impressive cathedral, with a substantially unaltered Gothic interior. It's dramatically high and simple inside, with elegant vaulting, beautiful windows and several fine tombs. The Christ sculpture, the *Senhor dos Passos,* is one of the main processional figures of the town's Easter celebrations. (Rua

da Sé; admission €1; ☉ 9am-12.30pm & 2-5pm Mon-Fri, plus 9am-1pm Sat Jun-Aug)

Museu Municipal de Arqueologia MUSEUM

3 Map p64, C3

Below the cathedral is the impressive, well laid out town archaeological museum. In the centre is a well-preserved 4m-wide, 18m-deep Moorish well surrounded by a spiral staircase, which was discovered during excavations. The museum exhibits prehistoric, Roman and Moorish antiquities and is built into a section of the Almohad town walls. Intriguing items include a huge 13th-century anchor and the skeleton of a young man felled by a crossbow bolt found during excavations in the castle. (☏ 282 444 838; Rua das Portas de Loulé; adult/under 10yr €2.10/free, joint ticket with Castelo €3.90; ☉ 10am-6pm)

Krazy World WATER PARK

4 Map p64, E3

Near São Bartolomeu de Messines, about 17km northwest of Silves, this animal and crocodile park also has minigolf, ponies and two swimming pools. It also offers transport from Albufeira. (☏ 282 574 134; www.krazyworld. com; Algoz; adult/child €13/8; ☉ 10am-6pm or 6.30pm Mar-Oct, plus most weekends Nov-Feb)

Igreja da Misericórdia CHURCH

5 Map p64, C2

The 16th-century Igreja da Misericórdia is plain apart from its distinctive,

The Cove of Carvoeiro

This diminutive seaside resort, 15km south of Silves, is a cluster of whitewashed buildings rising up above tawny, gold and green cliffs. Shops, bars and restaurants rise steeply from the small arc of beach that is the focus of the town, and other spectacular beaches are within easy reach. It is prettier and more laid-back than many of the bigger resorts, but its small size means that it gets full to bursting in summer.

fanciful Manueline doorway (not the main entrance), which is decorated with curious heads, pine cones, foliage and aquatic emblems. (Rua da Misericórdia; ⏰9am-1pm & 2-5pm Mon-Fri)

Country Riding Centre
HORSE RIDING

6 ◎ Map p64, E1

Located about 4km east of Silves, left off the road to Messines (it is signposted); offers lessons and hour-long to half-day rides at all levels. (☏917 976 992; www.countryridingcentre.com; 1/3hr ride €40/80)

Percurso dos Sete Vales Suspensos
WALKING

7 ◎ Map p64, D4

This spectacular cliff-top walk connects the beaches east of Carvoeiro. Beginning at Praia Vale Centianes, 2.3km east of town, it heads 5.7km to Praia da Marinha, with its picturesque rock stacks, via the beach at Benagil. It's one of the Algarve's most memorable walks.

Praia da Marinha
BEACH

8 ◎ Map p64, D4

One of a few beaches in the vicinity with karstic rock stacks, this is perhaps the most beautiful. As it's also a little harder to get to, it can be less crowded, though these things are relative in summer. It's 8km southeast of Lagoa, but the nicest way to get here is the Percurso dos Sete Vales Suspensos.

Slide & Splash
WATER PARK

9 ◎ Map p64, D4

This popular water park is situated 2km west of Lagoa. It's widely considered Portugal's best; kids and adults alike rave about the sheer quantity of attractions, including slides, toboggans and more. There's enough here to keep a family entertained for most of a day. (☏282 340 800; www.slidesplash.com; Estrada Nacional 125; adult/child 5-10yr €26/19; ⏰10am-5pm, 6pm or 6.30pm daily May-Sep, Mon-Sat Apr & Oct)

Divers Cove
DIVING

10 ◎ Map p64, D4

This multilingual family-run diving centre provides equipment, dives and Professional Association of Diving Instructors (PADI) certification. (☏282 356 594; www.divers-cove.com; Quinta do Paraíso; 3hr introduction €80, 1-day discovery €135, 2-day scuba diver €270, 4-day open water €450; ⏰9am-7pm)

Eating

Restaurante O Barradas
PORTUGUESE €€€

11 Map p64, D4

The star choice for foodies is this delightful converted farmhouse run by Luís and his German wife Andrea. They take pride in careful sourcing, and use organic fish, meat and fruits in season. Luís is a winemaker so you can be assured of some fine wines. To get there, follow the road to Lagoa and then to Palmeirinha; it's 3km from Silves. (☏282 443 308; www.obarradas.com; Palmeirinha; mains €8.50-25; ☺6-10pm Thu-Tue; 🏃)

Café Inglês
INTERNATIONAL €€

12 Map p64, C2

Located below the castle entrance, Café Ingles has a wonderful, shady terrace. The food is excellent (don't miss the chocolate St Emilion dessert). One of the liveliest restaurants north of the coast, it boasts an elegant interior, and has live jazz, fado and African music on weekends. (☏282 442 585; www.cafeingles.com; Rua do Castelo 11; mains €10-23; ☺9am-5.30pm Mon, to midnight Tue-Sun Mar-Oct; 🛜🖊)

Marisqueira Rui
SEAFOOD €€

13 Map p64, C3

Situated in the old town, with a comfortably dated interior of yellow and cork, this place is Silves' finest seafood restaurant. Join the locals – it gets busy – and savour plates from cockles, clams and crabs to bass and seafood rice. You can eat cheaply on bream or sea bass here, or blow the budget on a crustacean feast. (☏282 442 682; www.marisqueirarui.com; Rua Conselheiro Vilarinho 27; mains €9-18; ☺noon-11pm Wed-Mon)

Tasca Béné
PORTUGUESE €

14 Map p64, C3

This atmospheric traditional *tasca* (tavern) serves up all the Portuguese clichés – chequered cloths and old-world paraphernalia – and it's got a great reputation for doing so. The menu comprises daily meat and fish specials (€7.50), and by night it offers an à la carte menu. *Cataplanas* (seafood stews) are available for two. (☏282 444 767; Rua Policarpo Dias; mains €8-12; ☺10am-midnight Mon-Sat)

Pastelaria Rosa
PATISSERIE €

15 Map p64, C3

On the ground floor of the town-hall building, this quaint, tile-lined place is Silves' oldest cafe and the best place to try Algarvian sweets. (Largo do Município; pastries €1.50-3; ☺7.30am-10pm Mon-Sat; 🛜)

Recanto dos Mouros
PORTUGUESE €€

16 Map p64, C1

Situated a kilometre or so behind the castle (follow the signs), this is one of Silves' most popular places. As the Portuguese attest, it's *bom preço-qualidade* (damn good value) for lots of hearty Algarvian delights. (☏282 443 240; www.recantodosmouros.com;

Understand

Silves & the Moors

- -

The Muslim Conquest

In the 7th century AD, the teachings of Mohammed swept across North Africa and in 711, less than a century after the prophet's death, Iberia was invaded from Morocco, the kin-strife-plagued Visigoths deposed and most of the peninsula taken in only three years: an astonishing feat.

The Moorish domains in Iberia became known as Al-Andalus (from where we get the word Andalucía), and its western portion was referred to as Al-Gharb (the west), from which Algarve directly derives. Though they were pushed back gradually from the north of Spain and Portugal, the Moors were to rule the Algarve for over half a millennium.

Life Under Moorish Rule

Silves (Xelb or Shelb) was by far the most important town in the region, with a navigable river and a booming trade in nuts and dried fruit. After the disintegration of the dynasty that had ruled the region from Córdoba in Spain, it became its own city-state during the so-called *taifa* period of the 11th century.

For a long time, southerners enjoyed peace and prosperity under the Moors, who were – more or less – tolerant of Jews and Christians. They introduced many innovations in farming, architecture, science and crafts. Numerous Portuguese words – mostly connected with food and agriculture – and place names come from this time, easily recognised by the article 'al' or its derivatives, such as Albufeira, Aljezur, *azeitona* (olive), *arroz* (rice) or *alface* (lettuce). Another Moorish legacy is the flat-roofed house, originally used to dry almonds, figs and corn, and to escape the night heat.

The Reconquest

In the 12th century the Christian reconquest of Portugal, aided by crusading forces from northern Europe, was hotting up, and Silves was taken by Sancho I in 1189. But the Almohad dynasty hit back, and retook the town two years later. Silves then enjoyed another period in the sun, before it finally fell to the Christians in 1242. Its importance diminished after this, and, despite a 19th-century cork boom, once the river silted up Silves was destined to become the charming backwater you see today.

Carvoeiro (p66)

Monte Branco; mains €9-14; ⊙lunch & dinner Thu-Tue)

A Marisqueira
SEAFOOD €€

17 Map p64, D4

This simple, well-established place has an outdoor terrace and is known for its seafood and grilled dishes. It's about 500m up the main road east of Carvoeiro beach. (www.facebook.com/amarisqueira.carvoeiro; Estrada do Farol 95; mains €12-25; ⊙lunch & dinner Mon-Sat)

Drinking

Restaurante Boneca Bar
BAR

18 Map p64, D4

Hidden in the rock formations at Algar Seco, just over a kilometre east of Carvoeiro beach, this long-standing place is a novel location for a cocktail, a great spot to be at sunset and a decent place for a light meal or beer at any time. (☑282 358 391; www.facebook.com/restaurante bonecabar; ⊙10am-midnight Apr-Sep)

Shopping

Estudio Destra
CERAMICS

19 Map p64, C2

This studio in a historic building specialises in beautiful hand-painted tile panels, mostly done on commission. (☑922 230 414; www.studiotiles.net; Largo Jerónimo Osório; ⊙9.30am-5.30pm Mon-Sat)

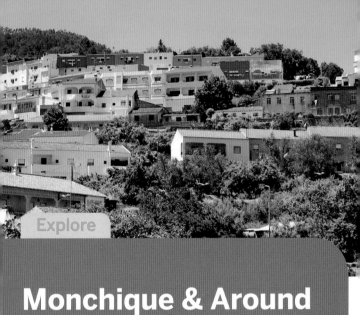

Explore

Monchique & Around

High above the coast, in cooler mountainous woodlands, the picturesque town of Monchique makes a lovely base for exploring the surrounding area, with some excellent options for walking, canoeing and biking. Neighbouring Caldas de Monchique, a sweet little spa hamlet, is another alluring factor, and the nearby peaks of Fóia and Picota are the Algarve's highest, offering splendid panoramas.

Region in a Day

Begin your day by driving up to **Fóia** (p75), the Algarve's highest point; the views are at their best in the morning light. From here, take the 6.5km loop walk before the heat of the sun gets too fierce.

After admiring the vistas one final time, head back down the hill, winding through cork groves towards Monchique, and stop for lunch at **O Luar da Fóia** (p76) for hearty traditional food in an inspiring setting.

The heat of the afternoon is a good time to explore the shady valley of Caldas de Monchique, perhaps relaxing in the **spa** (p75). In the late afternoon head back to Monchique itself and stroll its pretty streets, taking in the **Igreja Matriz** (p75) and the pottery workshop of **Leonel Telo** (p77). Toast an outstanding day with a drink at **Ó Chá Lá** (p76) or **Barlefante** (p77), before quality regional food at **A Charrete** (p76).

Top Experiences

Via Algarviana (p72)

Best of Monchique & Around

Outdoors
Via Algarviana (p72)

Fóia (p75)

Outdoor Tours (p75)

Alternativtour (p76)

Dining
A Charrete (p76)

O Luar da Fóia (p76)

Historic Architecture
Igreja Matriz (p75)

Cafes
Ó Chá Lá (p76)

Nightlife
Barlefante (p77)

Getting There

Bus Buses run here from Portimão, from where you can change to other Algarve destinations.

Top Experiences
Via Algarviana

If you like a good walk, by far the best way of appreciating the magnificent landscapes of the inland Algarve is to hike sections (or all) of this 300km trail that crosses the region from northeast to southwest. Some of the most beautiful sections are around Monchique, where splendid vistas open up as you climb through cork groves to the Algarve's highest hilltops.

👁 Map p74, B4

www.viaalgarviana.org

Don't Miss

Silves to Monchique

One of the Algarve's most satisfying day walks is this 28km section from historic Silves into the hilly interior and up Picota, the region's second-highest point. Great views are on offer, and the terrain of eucalyptus plantations and cork forest is picturesque throughout. It's a decent workout though, and you'll deserve a hearty meal once you reach Monchique. No shops en route.

Monchique to Fóia

The climb to Fóia (p75; pictured left) is an iconic Algarve rite of passage. Though no Everest at 902m, it offers magnificent perspectives over the whole southwestern coast. It's a steady rather than tough climb, emerging from eucalyptus groves into more exposed hill scenery. From the top you can head on to the verdant Penedo do Buraco gorge and from there to the hill village of Marmelete.

Salir to Alte

This section joins two of the main settlements of the picturesque Serra do Caldeirão (p52) and gives a good glimpse of the landscapes and ways of rural life of this inland Algarvian region. It's an easy 16km, with some decent rural eating options along the way.

Vila do Bispo to Cabo de São Vicente

The last section of the Via Algarviana is an easy 17km stage taking in interesting coastal landscapes, plenty of native and migratory bird life and ending at the bleak, stunning cape that marks the end of the Algarve, Portugal and Europe. It's a fitting finish to the trail. There's an alternative cliff-side route, part of the Rota Vicentina (p107).

☑ Top Tips

▶ You can download route information at www.viaalgarviana.org.

▶ The trail is reasonably well signposted, but there are some places where confusion is possible, particularly when crossing roads.

▶ Grabbing the GPS points off the website can be a big help.

▶ The Algarve's summer heat means that early starts make for happier walking.

▶ The best two-day taster of the trail is to stay in Monchique, walk up to Picota and back one day, and up to Fóia and back the next.

✗ Take a Break

Most sections of the trail have villages at pretty regular intervals, but make sure you're stocked up with snacks and water.

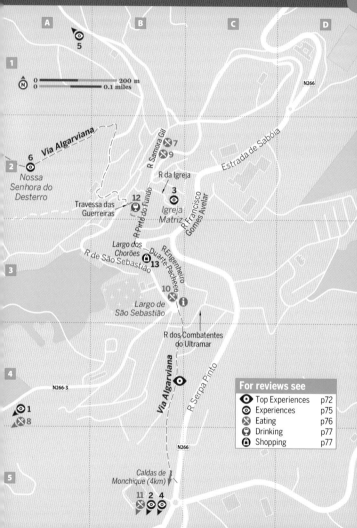

A B C D

5

N266

0   200 m
0   0.1 miles

Via Algarviana

6

Nossa Senhora do Desterro

R Samora Gil

7
9

R da Igreja

3

Igreja Matriz

Estrada de Sabóia

Travessa das Guerreiras

12

R Pinto do Fundo

R Francisco Gomes Avelar

Largo dos Chorões

R de São Sebastião

13

R Engenheiro Duarte Pacheco

10

Largo de São Sebastião

R dos Combatentes do Ultramar

N266-3

Via Algarviana

R Serpa Pinto

1
8

N266

Caldas de Monchique (4km)

11   2   4

For reviews see	
⦿ Top Experiences	p72
⊙ Experiences	p75
⊗ Eating	p76
⦿ Drinking	p77
🔒 Shopping	p77

Experiences

Fóia
HILL

1 Map p74, A4

The Algarve's highest point, 8km west of Monchique, this hill offers stunning views to the coast and beyond. The road climbs through cork and pine groves, which then open up to vast vistas over the rolling hills. On the way are numerous eating stops. Atop the hill is a forest of telecommunications masts and some desultory handicraft shops, but the perspectives are what you're here for. You can walk to the summit from Monchique; from the top, there are also marked loop trails of 6.5km and 17km.

Termas de Monchique Spa
SPA

2 Map p74, B5

In the wooded valley below town; admission allows access to the sauna, steam bath, gym, and swimming pool with hydromassage jets. You can then indulge in special treatments, from a Cleopatra bath to a chocolate-mask wrap. (📞282 910 910; www.monchiquetermas.com; admission €15, hotel guests €12; ⏱mid-Feb–Dec)

Igreja Matriz
CHURCH

3 Map p74, B2

The local church has an extraordinary, star-shaped Manueline porch decorated with twisted columns that look like lengths of knotted rope. The side door is also impressive. Inside you'll find a simple interior, with columns topped with ropey capitals, and a side chapel that contains beautiful 17th-century glazed tiles showing St Francis, sinners in hell, and St Michael roughing up the devil. Behind the church is a small **museum of sacred art** (www.cm-monchique.pt; Rua da Igreja; admission €1; ⏱10am-1pm Mon-Fri).

Outdoor Tours
OUTDOORS

4 Map p74, B5

This Dutch-run company offers biking (€29 to €48), kayaking (from Lagos; €30) and walking trips (day walk €38), both in and around the Algarve and

---

Understand
The Cork Harvest

Portugal produces about half of the world's cork, mostly in the Alentejo and Algarve. The light, flexible, waterproof bark of the mature cork oak (*sobreiro* in Portuguese) is stripped every nine years – a skilled manual procedure conducted in summer – to give us cork (*cortiça*) for tiles, anti-insect hats, footwear and wine-bottle stoppers. The trees grow the bark back and go on to live for several centuries. This, and the fact that cork groves offer both traditional grazing land and an important wildlife habitat, means that the cork industry is very sustainable – a fact that has boosted the cork's recent comeback against artificial wine-bottle stoppers.

Top Tip

Walks around Monchique

It's around 10.5km return to the top of Picota, and 8km one way to the summit of Fóia. There are several other reasonably well-marked walks in the vicinity.

Serra de Monchique. (☑282 969 520; www.outdoor-tours.com; Rua Francisco Bivar 142A, Mexilhoeira Grande; tours from €20)

Alternativtour
OUTDOORS

 5 Map p74, A1

Alternativtour runs mountain-biking tours, canoeing trips or combined mountain-biking and canoeing trips, and guided walks. Tours require a minimum of two people; per-person prices decrease the larger the group. Bike hire costs €20 per day. (☑965 004 337; www.alternativtour.com; tours €50-75)

Nossa Senhora do Desterro
CHAPEL

 6 Map p74, A2

Overlooking the town from a wooded hilltop are the ruins of the 17th-century Franciscan monastery. It is on the path of the Via Algarviana and you can climb up here.

Eating

A Charrete
PORTUGUESE €€

 7 Map p74, B2

Touted as the area's best eatery for its

wide menu of regional specialities, this likeably old-fashioned place serves reliably good cuisine amid country-rustic charm. A few favourites include cabbage with spicy sausages and an award-winning honey flan for dessert. (☑282 912 142; Rua Samora Gil 30-34; mains €11-15; ☺lunch & dinner Thu-Tue)

O Luar da Fóia
PORTUGUESE €€

 8 Map p74, A4

Gorgeous is the only word to use here for the setting (slightly rustic), the view (cliff-edge expansive) and the cuisine (full-on traditional Portuguese using quality produce). Chicken piri-piri is the go here, as is suckling pig, cow's cheek in a pot and some excellent-value wines. It's a kilometre from the Monchique *turismo* (tourist office) on the road to Fóia. (☑282 911 149; www.facebook.com/luardafoia; Estrada da Fóia; mains €7-13; ☺10am-11pm Tue-Sun)

Ó Chá Lá
CAFE €

 9 Map p74, B2

Tea houses are a bit like puppies: it's very difficult to dislike them. And this sweet spot is no exception, doing light meals such as soups and quiches, and turning out some excellent cakes and tarts in a bright, tiled-floor space. (Rua Samora Gil 12; light meals €2-6; ☺9am-7pm Mon-Fri, to 2pm Sat; 🛜🍴)

Restaurante O Parque
PORTUGUESE €

10 Map p74, B3

Directly opposite the Monchique tourist office, this cosy local haunt serves good, honest, down-to-earth dishes at green-clad, unsteady tables. Many workers head here for lunch. (Rua Engenheiro Duarte Pacheco 54; mains €7-13; ⊘lunch & dinner)

Restaurante 1692   RESTAURANT €€

This upmarket place has tables in the tree-shaded central square, and a classy interior, and is located in the Termas de Monchique Spa (see 2 ◎ Map p74, B5) complex. Service is a bit hit-and-miss, and the setting is perhaps a little better than the decent, but overpriced, food. (☏282 910 910; www.monchiquetermas.com; mains €9-18; ⊘lunch & dinner mid-Feb–Dec; 🛜)

Café Império   PORTUGUESE €

11 🍴 Map p74, B5

Locals flock to this place for what is reputedly the best piri-piri chicken in the region, with lovely views of the valley to boot. Heading north, it's 700m on the left-hand side past the turn-off to Caldas; look for the tiled 'Schweppes' sign on the wall. (☏282 912 290; N266; mains €6-12; ⊘lunch & dinner Wed-Mon; 🛜)

Drinking

Barlefante   BAR

12 🍺 Map p74, B2

Monchique's coolest haunt, this fun cavelike place has a touch of the burlesque, with hot pink walls, red-velvet alcoves, ornate mirrors and chandeliers. The outdoor tables on this narrow alley are also a prime spot. (www.facebook.com/barlefante; Travessa das Guerreiras; ⊘noon-2am Mon-Thu, 1pm-4am Fri & Sat, to 2am Sun; 🛜)

Shopping

Leonel Telo   CERAMICS

13 🔒 Map p74, B3

Now located on the main road, by the big bend in the centre of town, this studio lets you watch potter Leonel at work and browse his bright, quality ceramics. (Rua Engenheiro Duarte Pacheco; ⊘9am-2pm & 3-6pm Mon-Sat)

Explore

Lagos

Touristy, likeable Lagos lies on a riverbank, with 16th-century walls enclosing the old town's attractive cobbled streets. A huge range of restaurants and pumping nightlife add to the allure provided by fabulous beaches and numerous watery activities. Aside from its hedonistic appeal, Lagos has historical clout, having launched many naval excursions during Portugal's extraordinary Age of Discovery.

Region in a Day

For many, a day in Lagos starts with a hangover, so down a strong coffee in **Café Gombá** (p86) before exploring the old town. Visit the lovably higgledy-piggledy **Museu Municipal** (p83), including the baroque glory of the **Igreja de Santo António** (p83), and then the **Fortaleza da Ponta da Bandeira** (p83; pictured left), admiring the sturdy town walls along the way.

Take a cab to **Bar Quim** (p86) on Meia Praia and enjoy fish soup beachside. It's then a lovely walk back along the sand to the marina, where you should take a boat trip to see the coast or to spot dolphins. Once you've docked again, have a sundowner at **Upperdeck** (p88) on the marina's top level.

There are numerous options for dinner; try to get into the **Casinha do Petisco** (p85) or, for a more sedate meal, **Dom Vinho II** (p86). Afterwards, it depends on your taste: a stylish gin and tonic at **Taberna de Lagos** (p88), the surfer vibe at **Red Eye Bar** (p88) or backpacker debauchery at **The Tavern** (p88). Later, **Bon Vivant** (p87) is a great choice with its roof terrace and well-mixed cocktails, and everyone seems to end up at **Grand Café** (p88).

Top Experiences

On the Water (p80)

Best of Lagos

Getting There

Train Lagos is at the western end of the Algarve line, with frequent services along the coast to Faro.

Bus Buses head from Lagos to all of the Algarve's major towns, and further afield.

Top Experiences
On the Water

Lagos, set on a wide bay, offers numerous ways to get out on the water. There's a huge number of companies offering boat trips, which can focus on birdwatching, fishing, the striking coastal scenery or dolphin-spotting. Getting active is easy too, with every type of watery pursuit on offer, including diving, surfing, windsurfing, kiting, kayaking, paddleboarding and more.

Boat trips run all year, with departures in summer from 10am until the evening.

Kayaking near Lagos

Don't Miss

Dolphin-Watching

A popular excursion from Lagos offered by several tour outfits. You're very likely to spot common dolphins and bottlenose dolphins; Risso's dolphins, sea turtles and, occasionally, whales are also seen. (Most companies will offer a discount or a free trip the next day if you don't spot dolphins.) The trips are mostly in rigid inflatables designed to find dolphins fast, so don't expect a leisurely cruise.

Diving

The wide bay affords rewarding diving, with good rather than spectacular visibility. Expect to see rays, octopuses, colourful nudibranchs, moray eels and various crustaceans. There's an artificial reef off Alvor, which offers great fish-viewing; for expert divers, there are also some shipwrecks in the area. Several companies in Lagos offer courses, guided dives and equipment hire.

Windsurfing & Kiteboarding

The relatively calm waters of Meia Praia and regular winds make it a fine spot for windsurfing, particularly for beginners. Kiting is good here too, and even more so a little way to the east, off Alvor. Several companies offer these activities with both hire and classes available. Wakeboarding and water-skiing are also on offer.

Coastal Scenery

The limestone coast around Lagos has been weathered and eroded into some fabulous scenery. A huge range of boat trips is available in Lagos to cruise along the picturesque shore, taking in various caves and grottoes, but it's even more fun to explore yourself in a sea kayak or on a paddleboard.

☑ Top Tips

▶ Most of the boat-trip operators have stalls along the waterfront strip in Lagos, and also around the marina.

▶ Competition among boat-trip operators can be quite intense, and sometimes ticket vendors will stretch the truth a bit to get you on board their vessel. Be warned!

✗ Take a Break

Meia Praia is dotted with appealing eateries, so it's easy to hit the beach, eat, then head straight back to the water. Bar Quim (p86) is a classic Portuguese beachsider.

For a more upmarket seaside meal, nearby Atlântico (p85) is excellent.

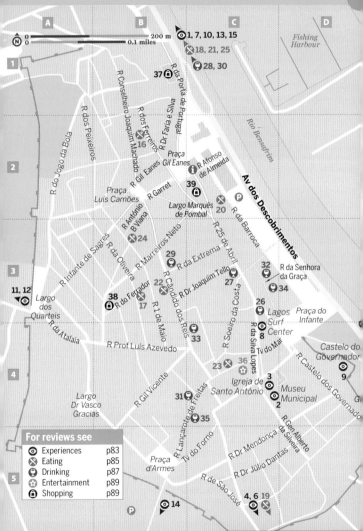

Fishing Harbour

1, 7, 10, 13, 15
18, 21, 25
28, 30
37
R da Porta de Portugal
R dos Peixeiros
R Conselheiro Joaquim Machado
R dos Ferreiros
R Dr Faria e Silva
R do Jogo da Bola
16
Praça Gil Eanes
R Afonso de Almeida
R Gil Eanes
Rio Bensafrim
Praça Luís Camões
R Garret
39
Av dos Descobrimentos
Largo Marquês de Pombal
20
R da Barroca
R António B Viana
24
R Infante de Sagres
R da Oliveira
R Marreiros-Neto
29
R da Extrema
R 25 de Abril
32
R da Senhora da Graça
34
11, 12
Largo dos Quartéis
38
R do Ferrador
22
17
R Cândido dos Reis
R Dr Joaquim Tello
27
R Soeiro da Costa
26
Lagos Surf Center
Praça do Infante
R da Atalaia
R I de Maio
33
8
Tv do Mar
Castelo do Governador
9
R Prof Luís Azevedo
23
36
Igreja de Santo António
3
Museu Municipal
2
R Castelo dos Governador
Largo Dr Vasco Gracias
R Gil Vicente
31
R Lançarote de Freitas
35
R da Silva Lopes
R Gen Alberto da Silveira
Praça d'Armes
Tv do Forno
R Dr Mendonça
R Dr Júlio Dantas
R de São José
4, 6
19
14

For reviews see

⊙ Experiences	p83
⊗ Eating	p85
⊗ Drinking	p87
⊕ Entertainment	p89
⊕ Shopping	p89

Experiences

Algarve Dolphins   BOAT TOUR

1 Map p82, B1

Offers dolphin-spotting trips in zippy rigid inflatables with marine biologists on board. (☏282 788 513; www.algarve-dolphins.com; adult/child from €35/25)

Museu Municipal   MUSEUM

2 Map p82, C4

Lagos' town museum, an old-fashioned but lovably eclectic and curious collection, holds a bit of everything: swords and pistols, landscapes and portraits, minerals and crystals, coins, china, miniature furniture, Roman mosaics, African artefacts, stone tools, model boats, and an intriguing model of an imaginary Portuguese town. The museum is also the entry point for the baroque Igreja de Santo António. (☏282 762 301; Rua General Alberto da Silveira; adult/concession €3/1.50; ⏰10am-12.30pm & 2-5.30pm Tue-Sun)

Igreja de Santo António   CHURCH

3 Map p82, C4

This little church, bursting with gilded, carved wood, is a stupendous baroque extravaganza. Beaming cherubs and ripening grapes are much in evidence. The dome and *azulejo* (hand-painted tiles) panels were installed during repairs after the 1755 earthquake. Enter the church from the adjacent Museu Municipal. (Rua General Alberto da Silveira; adult/child incl museum €3/1.50; ⏰10am-12.30pm & 2-5.30pm Tue-Sun)

Ponta da Piedade   VIEWPOINT

4 Map p82, C5

Protruding south from Lagos, Ponta da Piedade (Point of Piety) is a stunning, dramatic wedge of headland. Three windswept kilometres out of town, the point is well worth a visit for its contorted, polychrome sandstone cliffs and towers, complete with lighthouse and, in spring, hundreds of nesting egrets. The surrounding area is brilliant with wild orchids in spring. On a clear day you can see east to Carvoeiro and west to Sagres.

Fortaleza da Ponta da Bandeira   FORT

5 Map p82, D4

This petite fortress at the southern end of the avenue was built in the 17th century to protect the port. Now restored, it houses an exhibition on the Portuguese discoveries and a quaint chapel dedicated to Santa Barbara, often invoked as a protector against storms. (Av dos Descobrimentos; adult/concession €3/1.50; ⏰10am-12.30pm & 2-5.30pm Tue-Sun)

Blue Ocean   DIVING

6 Map p82, C5

For those who want to go diving or snorkelling, Blue ocean offers a half-day discovery experience (€30), a full-day dive (€90) and a divemaster Professional Association of Diving Instructors (PADI) scuba course (€590). It also offers kayak safaris (half-/full day €30/45, child under 12 years half-price). (☏964 665 667; www.blue-ocean-divers.de)

Riverwatch

BIRDWATCHING

7 Map p82, B1

The knowledgable skipper of this small operation runs worthwhile boat trips to the nearby Paúl de Lagos wetland area. (967 221 483; www.facebook.com/riverwatchlagos; trips €20)

Lagos Surf Center

SURFING

8 Map p82, C4

Will help you catch a wave and head to where there are suitable swells. Children must be accompanied by a family member over 14 years of age. It also rents out wetsuits (€5 per day) and boards (€15 to €25) and offers beach kayaking and paddleboarding trips. (282 764 734; www.lagossurfcenter.com; Rua da Silva Lopes 31; 1-/3-/5-day courses €55/150/225)

Castelo dos Governadores

CASTLE

9 Map p82, D4

Built by the Moors, Lagos' Governors Castle was conquered by Christian forces in the 13th century. It's said that the ill-fated, evangelical Dom Sebastião attended an open-air Mass here and spoke to the assembled nobility from a small Manueline window in the castle before leading them to a crushing defeat at Alcácer-Quibir (Morocco). Admire the window for as long as you can bear the urine smells from the previous night's party, then check out the nearby bastion and gateway.

Parque Zoológico de Lagos

ZOO

10 Map p82, B1

The zoo is a shady 3-hectare kid-pleaser, with small primates and a children's farm housing domestic animals. It's near the village of Barão de São João, 8km west of Lagos. (282 680 100; www.zoolagos.com; Quinta Figueiras; adult/child €16/12; 10am-7pm Apr-Sep, to 5pm Oct-Mar;)

Axessextreme

KAYAKING

11 Map p82, A3

Offers recommended sea-kayaking trips in the Algarve. Also offers mountain biking and surfing. (919 114 649; www.axessextreme.com; 3hr tour €25)

Tiffany's

HORSE RIDING

12 Map p82, A3

Seven kilometres west of Lagos, this outfit charges €33 for an hour's horse riding. Other options include a three-hour trip (€85), or a five-hour trip that includes a champagne picnic (€140). (282 697 395; www.teamtiffanys.com; Vale Grifo, Almádena; 9am-dusk)

Windsurf Point

WINDSURFING

13 Map p82, B1

Windsurfing courses (beginners full-day course €190) at Meia Praia, along with kite-surfing, paddleboarding, board rental (per hour/day €35/70) and a shop. (282 792 315; www.windsurfpoint.com; Bairro 1º Maio, Meia Praia; 9am-7pm)

Mountain Bike Adventure

CYCLING

14 Map p82, B5

Bike geeks will have some fun with this company, which offers a range of trips for all standards, from shorter scenic trips to full-on technical rides with shoots, drops and jumps. Also offers accommodation packages. (📞918 502 663; www.themountainbikeadventure.com; Porta da Vila; rides from €20)

Bom Dia

BOAT TOUR

15 Map p82, B1

The oldest operator, and based at the marina, Bom Dia runs trips on traditional schooners, including a five-hour barbecue cruise with a chance to swim (adult/child €49/25), a two-hour grotto trip (adult/child €22.50/10) or a family fishing trip (adult/child €35/25). (📞282 087 587; www.bomdia-boattrips.com)

Eating

A Forja

PORTUGUESE €€

16 Map p82, B2

The secret is out. This buzzing place pulls in the crowds – locals, tourists and expats – for its hearty, top-quality traditional food served in a bustling environment at great prices. Plates of the day are always reliable, as are the fish dishes. (📞282 768 588; Rua dos Ferreiros 17; mains €8-15; ⏰noon-3pm & 6.30-10pm Sun-Fri)

Understand

The 1755 Earthquake

The huge seismic shock that hit Portugal in 1755 is usually known as the Lisbon earthquake, due to the massive damage and loss of life in the country's capital, but its epicentre was actually 200km southwest of the Algarve. The region was devastated by the approximately 8.7-magnitude quake, and what was left along the coast was battered by the ensuing tsunami. Very few buildings survive from the pre-earthquake period, and those that did weather the quake usually needed extensive reconstruction. The Algarve is, hence, very rich in baroque architecture.

Casinha do Petisco

SEAFOOD €€

17 Map p82, B3

Blink (or be late) and you'll miss this tiny traditional gem. It's cosy and simply decorated and comes highly recommended for its seafood grills and shellfish dishes. (Rua da Oliveira 51; mains €7-13; ⏰6-11pm Mon-Sat)

Atlântico

PORTUGUESE €€€

18 Map p82, C1

Head to Meia Praia to experience this place, where the owner is a character and the quality is high. There's a bar, a stunning terrace with beach views and a very old wine collection. The menu, with both Portuguese and international dishes, is extensive. An excellent retreat. (📞 282 792 806; www.restauranteatlantico.com; Estrada da Meia Praia; mains €14-29; 🕐 lunch & dinner Mon-Sat; 🛜)

O Camilo
SEAFOOD €€

21 Map p82, C5

Just north of Ponta da Piedade, perched on the cliffs above pretty Praia do Camilo, this place is synonymous with seafood dishes (the selection is overseen by the restaurant patriarch). Seafood specialities are on offer daily. The setting is light, bright and airy, and has a large terrace. Definitely the place to linger. (Praia do Camilo; mains €8-15; 🕐 10am-10pm; 🛜)

Arribalé
GRILL HOUSE €€

20 Map p82, C2

Tucked away on Lagos' loveliest street, this supercompact place offers a short, simple menu of mostly salads and grilled meat. The owners are exceedingly friendly, quality is very high and there's an appealing, homely vibe here. There aren't many tables, so it's worth booking. (📞 918 556 618; www.arribale.com; Rua da Barroca 40; mains €11-19; 🕐 dinner Tue-Sat)

Local Life
Fresh-Baked

Lagos' oldest bakery, **Padaria Central** (Map p82, B3; Rua 1 de Maio 29; snacks from €1.30; 🕐 6.30am-8pm Mon-Fri, to 7pm Sat), has been here since 1906 and still bakes the freshest goods in the Algarve. It's great for early risers or partygoers who've seen the sun rise.

Bar Quim
PORTUGUESE €

21 Map p82, C1

Perhaps the best of the sandside eateries on Meia Praia, this is a fair stroll along the beach, but well worth it for the welcoming service, delicious fish soup and toothsome prawns sizzled in butter and garlic. (mains €7-12; 🕐 10am-10pm Fri-Wed; 🛜)

Café Gombá
CAFE €

22 Map p82, B3

This place has been around since 1964 and the friendly owner has a loyal local clientele who come for the coffee and the cakes, all baked on the premises. (📞 282 762 188; Rua Cândido dos Reis 56; 🕐 8am-7pm Mon-Sat, plus Sun mid-Jun–mid Sep; 🛜)

Dom Vinho II
PORTUGUESE €€

23 Map p82, C4

Removed from the main street bustle where its parent restaurant stands, this elegant upstairs dining area boasts solid dark wooden furniture and a refined feel. Service is truly excellent, and there's a top list of vintage wines. The food is competent rather than brilliant, but the overall package is great. There's a reduced menu after 11pm. (Rua Caçarote de Freitas 18; mains €11-20; 🕐 12.30pm-1.30am Mon-Sat, 7pm-1.30am Sun; 🛜)

Mimar Café
CAFE €

24 Map p82, B3

One of the town's best-value casual eateries, Mimar is excellent for coffees and breakfasts, plus home-baked meals

Bon Vivant

(accompanied by scrumptious salads). Daily luncheon specials are great deals for around €4. By night it's a tapas-cum-wine bar. (Rua António Barbosa Viana 27; snacks €3-8; ☺8am-midnight Mon-Sat Jun-Aug, to 10pm Sep-May; ☜)

Adega da Marina   PORTUGUESE €€

25 Map p82, C1

This barnlike place is a bit like a Portu-guese grandmother: she hasn't changed her hairstyle in a while, but she still dishes out generous portions of reliable (and economical) grilled chicken and seafood favourites to grateful guests (who queue to eat here in summer). Her accessories include iron chandeliers and farming implements. (☎282 764 284; www.

adegadamarina.grupoadm.pt; Av dos Descobri-mentos 35; mains €6-15; ☺noon-2am; ☜)

Drinking

Bon Vivant   BAR

26 ☻ Map p82, C3

This long-standing, central bar is far classier than some of the nearby options, takes some care over its mainly R&B mu-sic and makes an effort to keep patrons entertained. Spread across several levels with various terraces, Bon Vivant shakes up some great cocktails and is pretty hot once it gets going (usually late). Look out for bartenders' impressive juggling feats. (www.facebook.com/bonvivant.lagos; Rua 25 de Abril 105; ☺2pm-4am; ☜)

Taberna de Lagos
BAR

27 📍 Map p82, C3

Boasting a stylish space and brooding electronic music in a historic central building, this airy and atmospheric bar and restaurant attracts a somewhat savvier bargoer than the typical Lagos drinking den (higher cocktail prices also keep some punters away). It has live fado on Monday nights. (www.tabernalagos.pt; Rua Dr Joaquim Tello 1; ⏱noon-2am; 📶)

Duna Beach Club
BAR

28 📍 Map p82, C1

Chill out with the smart set at this hotel bar-restaurant, open day and night. It's located bang on Meia Praia beach, with a pool and attitude. At night it's the bar for the 'resort-chic' folk. (📞282 762 091; www.facebook.com/dunabeachlagos; Meia Praia; ⏱bar 9pm-2am, restaurant hours vary; 📶)

Red Eye Bar
BAR

29 📍 Map p82, B3

This straight-up rock and surf bar makes a top spot to kick off the night, with drinks specials, a pool table and friendly staff. (www.redeyebarlagos.com; Rua Cándido dos Reis 63; ⏱8pm-2am Tue-Sun)

Upperdeck
CAFE, BAR

30 📍 Map p82, C1

Run by a yacht charter company, this small bar upstairs at the marina has a lightly worn nautical theme and makes a very pleasant spot to sit and watch the boats below. It serves a short menu of burgers and the like. (www.facebook.com/upperdecklagos; Marina de Lagos; ⏱9am-2am; 📶)

The Tavern
BAR

31 📍 Map p82, C4

The Tavern is brassy and fun, luring backpackers with beer bongs, drinks promos, haggis shots (Jägermeister and Irn-Bru, since you asked) and the infamous Walk the Plank. (www.tavernlagos.com; Rua Lançarote de Freitas 34; ⏱10pm-4am)

Grand Café
CLUB

32 📍 Map p82, C3

This classy place has three bars, and lots of gold leaf, kitsch, red velvet and cherubs, over which are draped dressed-up local and foreign hipsters. Given its central location, it's a popular spot to end up. (Rua da Senhora da Graça; ⏱10pm-6am; 📶)

Inside Out
BAR

33 📍 Map p82, C4

This late-opener has good DJs and a lively atmosphere fuelled by enormous fishbowl cocktails. (www.facebook.com/insideoutFace; Rua Cândido dos Reis 19; ⏱8pm-4am; 📶)

Stevie Ray's Blues Jazz Bar
BAR

34 📍 Map p82, C3

This intimate two-level candlelit joint is the best live-music bar in town. On weekends it has live blues, jazz and oldies. It attracts a smart-casual older crowd. Admission is free, but there's a €5 minimum consumption applied. (www.stevie-rays.com; Rua da Senhora da Graça 9; ⊙Tue-Sat 9pm-4am; 🛜)

Garden
BEER GARDEN

 35 🍺 Map p82, C4

This appealingly decorated beer garden makes a great spot to lounge around on a sunny afternoon with a beer or cocktail. Once you smell the barbecuing meat, you might decide to stay for a meal, too. (Rua Lançarote de Freitas 29; ⊙10am-midnight Tue-Sun; 🛜)

Entertainment

Centro Cultural
CULTURAL CENTRE

 36 ⭐ Map p82, C4

This is Lagos' main venue for performances and contemporary-art exhibitions. (📞282 770 450; www.cm-lagos.pt; Rua Lançarote de Freitas 7; ⊙10am-8pm; 🛜)

Shopping

Mercado Municipal
MARKET

 37 🔒 Map p82, B1

Lagos' characterful municipal market is an intriguing place to wander, and a

Top Tip

Ordering a Beer

Now you're in Lagos, you need to know how to order a beer! For a small draught lager (200ml to 250ml), ask for *um fino* or *uma imperial*. *Uma caneca* is a bigger one (500ml). Ask for *uma cerveja* and you'll get a bottle (330ml), also called *uma média*. A little bottle (200ml) is *uma mini*.

great spot to stock up on fresh produce, including excellent seafood. (Av dos Descobrimentos; ⊙7am-2pm Mon-Sat)

Owl Story
BOOKS

38 🔒 Map p82, B3

Owl Story has an excellent supply of new and secondhand English books as well as sailing almanacs and boating books. (📞917 414 386; Rua Marreiros Neto 67; ⊙10am-5.30pm Mon-Fri, to 3pm Sat)

Little Beats
FOOD, DRINK

39 🔒 Map p82, C2

This friendly, central shop deals in a carefully selected range of gourmet products from around the country, including oils, wines, some interesting artisanal beers and more. (Rua Afonso de Almeida 14; ⊙11am-5pm Mon-Sat)

Explore

Sagres & Around

The small, elongated village of Sagres, with a rich nautical history, has an end-of-the-world feel with its sea-carved coastline and cliff-top fortress. It also appeals for its access to fine beaches and water-based activities; it's especially popular, particularly in the last decade, with a surfing crowd. Outside town, the striking cliffs of Cabo de São Vicente make for an enchanting visit.

Region in a Day

☼ Stroll down to the port area and watch the morning action. The catch is auctioned off at the *lota* building near the breakwater. Browse the boat trips available here and perhaps book something for the late afternoon. Then head to the **fortaleza** (p92) and spend the rest of the morning exploring the headland behind the imposing walls.

☼ After lunch at **A Sagres** (p99) by the roundabout near the fortress, walk or drive the 5km to **Cabo de São Vicente** (p94). Admire the stark scenery and take in the small **Museu dos Faróis** (p95) before wandering back to town and getting out on the water. If you didn't fancy that, spend a couple of hours on one of the beaches, perhaps pretty **Martinhal** (p97).

☽ You might want to head back to Cabo de São Vicente to watch the sun set into the Atlantic Ocean. In town, dine on the delicious Portuguese fare at **A Casinha** (p98) before hitting the strip of bars on **Rua Comandante Matoso** (p100) for cocktails and revelry.

◉ Top Experiences

Fortaleza de Sagres (p92)

Cabo de São Vicente (p94)

♥ Best of Sagres & Around

Water Activities

Mar Ilimitado (p97)

DiversCape (p97)

Sagres Natura (p97)

Dining

A Casinha (p98)

Mum's (p98)

Nightlife

Agua Salgada (p100)

Warung (p100)

Outdoors

Walkin'Sagres (p97)

Getting There

🚍 **Bus** Buses run to Sagres from Lagos, the closest train station, and Portimão.

🚶 **Walking** Cabo de São Vicente is the terminus of the long-distance Via Algarviana and Rota Vicentina hiking routes.

Top Experiences
Fortaleza de Sagres

Muscular and seriously imposing from outside, this functional fortress occupies a large, mostly bare promontory, which offers breathtaking views over the sheer cliffs, and along the coast to Cabo de São Vicente. According to legend, this is where Prince Henry the Navigator established his navigation school and primed the early Portuguese explorers. The fortress buildings are interesting, but it's the walk around the headland that's the memorable part of the visit.

◉ Map p96, A3

www.monumentosdoalgarve.pt/pt/monumentos-do-algarve/fortaleza-de-sagres

☎ 282 620 140

adult/child €3/1.50

🕑 9.30am-8pm May-Sep, to 5.30pm Oct-Apr

Rosa dos Ventos

Don't Miss

The Bastions

Most of what you see today dates from a late-18th-century rebuilding of an earlier fort. Enter via the Porta da Praça, which formerly had a moat and drawbridge; on either side, the chunky Santo António and Santa Bárbara bastions allowed for a powerful crossfire.

Rosa dos Ventos

Inside the gate is a huge, curious stone pattern that measures nearly 50m in diameter. Named the *rosa dos ventos* (literally a 'pictorial representation of a compass'), this strange paving is believed to be a mariner's compass or a sundial of sorts. The paving may date from Prince Henry's time, but is more likely 16th century.

A Petite Church

The small whitewashed church of Nossa Senhora da Graça dates from 1570 and sits within the Sagres fortress precinct. It is a simple barrel-vaulted structure with a gilded 17th-century altarpiece. The bell tower was built over the former charnel house of the cemetery.

The Circuit Walk

The highlight of a visit to the fortress is the circular walk (or cycle) around the headland, with spectacular coastal views the reward. At the far end, near the lighthouse, don't miss the limestone crevices descending to the sea, or the labyrinth art installation by Portugal's famous sculpture-architect Pancho Guedes.

Cliff Fishing

Another intriguing aspect of the headland stroll is watching locals fishing off the cliffs. Though it's not a pastime you'd want to mention to your life insurers, you'll regularly see them pulling in grouper, turbot, bream or sea bass.

☑ Top Tips

▶ The tour buses roll in midmorning and after lunch, so get there early, lunchtime or late to avoid the groups.

▶ It's a long, exposed walk around the headland, so wear sunscreen and take plenty of water.

▶ Pack a pair of binoculars, too; there's plenty of bird life, and you've a chance of spotting dolphins and whales from the cliff tops.

✗ Take a Break

One of the best-value restaurants in Sagres is back at the roundabout turn-off for the fortress. A Sagres (p99) excels in seafood and daily specials.

Top Experiences
Cabo de São Vicente

Five kilometres from Sagres, Europe's south-westernmost point is a barren, thrusting headland that was the last piece of home that nervous Portuguese sailors would have seen as they launched into the unknown. It's a spectacular spot – revered even in the time of the Phoenicians. Known to the Romans as Promontorium Sacrum, it takes its present name from a Spanish priest martyred by the Romans. There's a lighthouse here, with a worthwhile museum, but the real attractions are the cliffs and the long, long view.

◉ Map p96, A1

⏲ lighthouse complex 10am-6pm Tue-Sun Apr-Sep, to 5pm Oct-Mar

Don't Miss

The Lighthouse Complex

The buildings at the cape have had a rough time of it over the years: as if the blustery conditions weren't enough, the 16th-century convent and fortress here were trashed by Sir Francis Drake in 1587, then largely demolished by the 1755 earthquake. The current lighthouse was built in 1846, is named Dom Fernando and has been automated since 1982.

Museu dos Faróis

In the lighthouse complex, this small, but excellent **museum** (adult/child €1.50/1; ⏲10am-6pm Tue-Sun Apr-Sep, to 5pm Oct-Mar) gives a good overview of Portugal's maritime navigation history, displays navigational instruments and replica folios of a 1561 atlas, and gives information on the history of the lighthouse. The info is well translated into English and gives an idea of the importance of Sagres during the Age of Discovery.

The Sunset

Standing here on the cliffs at the end of Europe and watching the sun set into the Atlantic Ocean is one of the Algarve's special experiences. You can almost hear the hissing as the orb hits the water...

Fortaleza do Beliche

A kilometre before reaching the lighthouse, you'll pass the Fortaleza do Beliche, built in 1632 on the site of an older fortress. The interior, once a hotel, is off limits, but you can go through the walls to the seaward side and descend a pretty pathway down to near the water. The sheltering walls here make for a more appealing picnic spot than the wind-whipped cape.

☑ Top Tips

▶ The area around the lighthouse can get pretty crowded with tourists, but walk a little way along the cliffs and you'll soon find a more serene end-of-Europe moment to have to yourself.

▶ Wonder where those ships are going? Log onto www.marinetraffic.com and find out.

▶ The telescopes here take €0.50 or €1 coins.

▶ Grab one of the window pews in the shop by the lighthouse and enjoy a beer – Sagres, of course – with a view.

✗ Take a Break

Simple snacks are available within the complex at the courtyard cafe or souvenir shop. Various fast-food stalls are lined up in the parking area outside.

By far the best option for a meal is to bring a picnic from Sagres, though finding a spot to shelter from the wind can be tricky.

Cabo de
São Vicente

Praia do
Tonel

Sítio do
Tonel

R São
Vicente

R do Mercado

Praia da
Baleeira

Porto da
Baleeira

Ponta da
Baleeira

R Dom
Sebastião

R da Moreta

R Comandante Matoso

R P António Faustino

Sagres
Surfcamp

Free Ride
Sagres

1 Mar-Ilimitado
5 Cape Cruiser
6 Sea Xplorer Sagres
2 DiversCape

8

3 12

14

7 Sensations
Wave

11

R Infante Dom Henrique

16

10

15

9

Praça da
República

Sagres
Natura 4

R da Fortaleza

Praia da
Mareta

ATLANTIC
OCEAN

Fortaleza
de Sagres

Ponta da

For reviews see	
◉ Top Experiences	p92
◎ Experiences	p97
✕ Eating	p98
◑ Drinking	p100

0   500 m
0   0.25 miles

Experiences

Mar Ilimitado
BOAT TOUR

1 Map p96, D1

Mar Ilimitado, a team of marine biologists, offers a variety of highly recommended, ecologically sound boat trips, from dolphin-spotting (€32; 1½ hours) and seabird-watching (€45; 2½ hours) to excursions up to Cabo de São Vicente (€25; one hour). (✆916 832 625; www.marilimitado.com; Porto da Baleeira)

Walkin'Sagres
WALKING TOUR

Multilingual Ana Carla offers recommended guided walks in the Sagres area, explaining the history and other details of the surrounds. The walks head through pine forests to the Cape's cliffs, and vary from shorter 6km options (€25; three hours) to a longer 8km walk (€40; 4½ hours). There's also a weekly walk for parents with young children (€15, children free). (✆925 545 515; www.walkinsagres.com)

Top Tip

Transport Hire
A useful place to get you mobile and ready to explore the area, centrally located **Maretta Shop** (✆282 624 535; www.marettashop.com; Rua Comandante Matoso; ◷9.30am-10.30pm) rents bikes (day hire €8 to €15), scooters, cars and more.

DiversCape
DIVING

2 Map p96, D1

Diving centres are based at the port. Recommended is the PADI-certified DiversCape, which organises snorkelling expeditions (€25, two hours), plus dives of between 12m and 30m around shipwrecks. (✆965 559 073; www.diverscape.com; Porto da Baleeira)

Praia do Martinhal
BEACH

3 Map p96, D1

One of the prettier beaches in the Sagres area, Martinhal is backed by a resort development, so is a little complex to find by car, but it's an easy walk from central Sagres. The water is calm and the angle of entry shallow, so it's a good one for families. Boat trips from Sagres harbour visit the pretty little limestone islands offshore.

Sagres Natura
SURFING

4 Map p96, B2

This recommended surf school also rents out bodyboards (€10 per day), surfboards (€15) and wetsuits (€5). It also offers canoeing trips (€35) and has bikes for hire (€15). (✆282 624 072; www.sagresnatura.com; Rua São Vicente)

Cape Cruiser
BOAT TOUR

5 Map p96, D1

Offers a range of boat trips, including dolphin-watching (€32, 1½ hours), seabird-watching (€45, 2½ hours), trips to Cabo São Vicente (€20, one hour), and various fishing excursions. (☎919 751 175; www.capecruiser.org; Porto da Baleeira)

Sea Xplorer Sagres   BOAT TOUR

 6 Map p96, D1

Leaving from the harbour in Sagres, this operator offers boat trips including dolphin-watching (€22, two hours), fishing (€45, four hours) or the cliffs of Cabo São Vicente from the sea (1½ hours, €20). (☎282 625 059; www.sea xplorersagres.com; Porto da Baleeira)

Wave Sensations   SURFING

7 Map p96, D1

Offers a range of lessons in surfing and paddleboarding, rents equipment and offers packages including accommodation at the Casa Azul hotel. (☎282 625 154; www.wavesensations.pt; Rua Comandante Matoso)

Free Ride Sagres Surfcamp   SURFING

8 Map p96, D1

One of several surf schools in the area, this set-up offers lessons, packages

Local Life
Local Eats

There's a cluster of good value, more typically Portuguese restaurants on and around Rua Comandante Matoso (Map p96, D1) just before it reaches the harbour.

and hire, as well as free transport from Sagres and Lagos to wherever the surf's good that day. (☎918 755 401, 916 089 005; www.freeridesurfcamp.com; Hotel Memmo Baleeira ; 1/3/5-day lessons €55/150/225)

Eating

A Casínha   PORTUGUESE €€

 9 Map p96, B2

This cosy terracotta-and-white spot – built on the site of the owner's grandparents' house – serves up some fabulous Portuguese cuisine, including standout barbecued fish, a good variety of *cataplanas* (seafood stews) for two (€34) and *arroz de polvo* (octopus rice). High quality, with a pleasant atmosphere. (☎917 768 917; www.facebook. com/acasinha.restaurantesagres; Rua de São Vicente; mains €12-18; ☺dinner Mon, lunch & dinner Tue-Sat)

Mum's   INTERNATIONAL €€

 10 Map p96, C1

Warm and cozy, eclectically decorated and friendly: that's the buzz at Sagres' latest favourite. The food – mostly vegetarian with some seafood – is delicious, wholesome and served with a smile. It has a good wine list and the staff are happy to recommend matches. It stays open for drinks after the kitchen closes. Best to book. No cards. (☎968 210 411; www.mums-sagres.com; Rua Comandante Matoso; mains €10-18; ☺food 7pm-midnight; 🛜🖋)

Understand
The Raven Saint

Although little is known about the life of São Vicente (St Vincent), his death was so legendary that both Spain and Portugal claim him.

A Spanish preacher martyred by the Romans in 304, Vicente was so remarkably composed during his burning at the stake, praising God in dulcet tones, that he converted several of his torturers. Though Spain says different, Portugal claims that his remains washed up near Sagres, in a boat watched over by two ravens. His shrine, which Muslim chronicles name as the Crow Church, became an object of Christian pilgrimage until its destruction by Muslim fanatics in the 12th century. Afonso Henriques, Portugal's first king, had the remains moved by ship to Lisbon in 1173, again accompanied by ravens. Vicente became Lisbon's patron saint; a raven features in its coat of arms.

The boat story can be seen as a fable used to Christianize what had already been a sacred site for centuries. The Romans called the area Promontorium Sacrum (from which Sagres' name derives), and there was an important temple to Saturn here.

Vila Velha INTERNATIONAL €€€

11 Map p96, D2

In a house with a lovely garden in front, the upmarket Vila Velha offers consistently good seafood mains, rabbit, grilled salmon and good vegetarian dishes. It has an international flavour; not for those who want 'real' Portuguese food. (☑282 624 788; www.vilavelha-sagres.com; Rua Patrão António Faustino; mains €16-30; �
dinner Tue-Sun; ☑)

Nortada PIZZERIA, SEAFOOD €

12 Map p96, D1

Rather charmingly set on the white-sand resort-backed Martinhal beach, this cute wooden shack has indoor and outdoor seating and serves up decent burgers and pizzas, as well as a few pricier seafood dishes. It's a relaxing spot. (☑918 613 410; www.restaurantenortada.com; Praia do Martinhal; pizzas €7-10; ☑10am-10pm; ☜✦)

A Sagres PORTUGUESE €€

13 Map p96, B1

This popular local restaurant offers great fish (such as *massinha do mar* for two, €28) and grilled meat fare that won't break the bank. It's on the roundabout as you turn off to the fort. (☑282 624 171; www.restauranteasagres.com; Av Infante Dom Henrique; mains €8-13; ☑lunch & dinner Thu-Tue)

A Grelha PORTUGUESE €€

14 Map p96, D1

Simple and likeable, this is one of a string of Portuguese restaurants on the street above the port. It doesn't do daily specials, but turns out competent and tasty fish and meat dishes in a cool, friendly atmosphere. (Rua Comandante Matoso; mains €8-12; ⏱lunch & dinner Mon-Sat)

Drinking

Agua Salgada CAFE, BAR

Situated in a strip of cafe-bars (see 16 ☻ Map p96, C1), Agua Salgada has good crêpes and is one of the liveliest at night, with DJs and a party mood. (☏282 624 297; Rua Comandante Matoso; ⏱10am-late; 📶)

Warung BAR

15 Map p96, C1

This popular postsurf spot plays a good variety of music, does decent food, offers a range of drinks and has a relaxed but upbeat atmosphere. Worth seeking out. (☏282 624 432; www.warung.eu; Rua do Mercado; ⏱6pm-2am; 📶)

Pau de Pita CAFE

The funkiest of its neighbours (see 16 ☻ Map p96, C1), at least in its design (think disco ball for tasteful mood lighting), this place has great salads, crêpes and juices (snacks €4 to €10) and plays

☑ Top Tip

Après-Surf Spots

A closely packed string of surfer-oriented places on Rua Comandante Matoso offers a bit of everything, whether it's a coffee or a caipirinha you're after; they are cafes by day, restaurants serving international favourites whatever time hunger drags you away from the beach, and lively bars by night.

pleasant house music. At night, it mixes decent drinks and is one of the liveliest bars on this strip. (Rua Comandante Matoso; ⏱10am-2am; 📶)

Dromedário CAFE, BAR

16 Map p96, C1

The legitimate founder of such cafe-bars, and still going strong (it's been here for over 30 years); good food, karaoke and 'mixology', aka creative cocktails. It's a fine spot, and it'll bring you in pizza from its sister restaurant out the back. (☏282 624 219; www. dromedariosagres.com; Rua Comandante Matoso; ⏱10am-late; 📶)

Mitic CAFE

This cafe is popular for its hefty toasted sandwiches (snacks €4 to €10), good cocktails and friendly environment, in a great location (see 16 ☻ Map p96, C1). (Rua Comandante Matoso; ⏱10am-late; 📶)

Understand
Prince Henry the Navigator & Sagres

The third son of King João I (whose defeat of the Castilian army at Aljubarrota achieved the stability that launched Portugal on the road to imperial power) Infante Dom Henrique (1394–1460), known in English as Prince Henry the Navigator, is a towering figure in Portuguese history and intimately connected to Lagos, Sagres and the whole Algarve.

Henry & the Algarve
Partly funded by his position as grand master of the Order of Christ (formerly known as the Templars), Henry built at Sagres a new, fortified town and a semimonastic school of navigation that specialised in cartography, astronomy and ship design.

At least, that's according to a difficult-to-unravel blend of history and myth. Henry was, among other things, governor of the Algarve and had a residence in its primary port town, Lagos, where he had ships built and crewed, and from where most expeditions set sail. He certainly did put together a kind of nautical think tank, though how much thinking went on out at Sagres is uncertain. He definitely had a house somewhere in or near Sagres, where he died in November 1460.

The Expeditions
In any event, the expeditions commissioned by Henry advanced further into the Atlantic and down the African coast. The sea route to west Africa brought much wealth to Portugal and the Algarve; trade with this region had previously been a monopoly of the trans-Saharan caravans. Unhappily, Henry's expeditions also marked the beginning of what we would now call colonialism, as well as the European slave trade in Africa. It's also likely that Henry's expeditions discovered, or at least suspected the existence of, the South American continent that was not officially reached by Portuguese until the 'discovery' of what is now Brazil by Pedro Álvares Cabral in 1500.

Drake then Earthquake
In May 1587 the English privateer Sir Francis Drake, in the course of attacking supply lines to the Spanish Armada, captured and wrecked the fortifications around Sagres. The town, one of the closest points to the epicentre, was then thoroughly destroyed in the 1755 earthquake.

Explore

West Coast Beaches

On the Algarve's western coast you'll find some amazing beaches, backed by beautiful wild vegetation. Much of this area is protected by the Parque Natural do Sudoeste Alentejano e Costa Vicentina, an important plant habitat and home to otters, foxes, wildcats and birds. The area has excellent surf conditions. Three appealingly small towns – Odeceixe, Aljezur and Carrapateira – are the main settlements.

Region in a Day

 Nothing clears the head like a bit of sea air, so head south from pretty Odeceixe to **Praia da Amoreira** (p107), one of our favourite beaches, for a cup of coffee and a look at what the surf's doing today. Once you've had your fill, head for Carrapateira, then take on the circular walk around **Praia da Bordeira** (p107; pictured left) **& Praia do Amado** (p107), with spectacular panoramas the whole way.

Both beaches have excellent eating options, so choose between **Sítio do Forno** (p111) or **Sítio do Rio** (p110) for lunch. When you get back to town, reward yourself with a cold beer at **Microbar Carrapateira** (p111), then visit the excellent **Museu do Mar** (p108) high above the town. On your way back to Aljezur, take the turn-off to **Praia de Vale Figueira** (p107) and feel the sand between your toes.

It's an atmospheric stroll up to the **castle** (p109) in Aljezur in the evening light; down below, the dinnertime atmosphere is great at **Pont'a Pé** (p110), with the smell of grilling fish accompanying surfers' tales of the wave that got away. Nightlife is limited outside summer, though at **Arrifana** (p107) there's always something going on.

Top Experiences

Surfing the West Coast (p104)

Best of the West Coast Beaches

Beaches
Praia de Odeceixe (p108)

Praia da Amoreira (p107)

Praia do Monte Clérigo (p109)

Praia da Arrifana (p107)

Praia de Vale Figueira (p107)

Praia da Bordeira & Praia do Amado (p107)

Museums
Museu Municipal (p109)

Museu do Mar e da Terra da Carrapateira (p108)

Water Activities
Arrifana Surf School (p108)

Algarve Surf School (p108)

Odeceixe Surf School (p108)

Getting There

Bus Buses run from Lagos to the three major settlements in this region: Carrapateira, Aljezur and Odeceixe.

Top Experiences
Surfing the West Coast

The Algarve's west coast is a world away from the packed resorts of the south. Big, handsome beaches offer decent beach breaks and a handful of excellent point breaks. When conditions are right, the mighty Atlantic rolls in some big waves; the concentration of differently faced beaches in a comparatively small area means that, with transport, you have a great chance of finding excellent surf.

Praia do Amado (p107)

Don't Miss

Carrapateira
With two excellent surf beaches, Praia da Bordeira and Praia do Amado (p107), within walking distance of town, this is a great spot to base yourself. The southern beach, Praia do Amado, offers a reliable year-round beach break and is long enough not to get overcrowded. Praia da Bordeira is also long and dependable, though beware of rocks on some entries.

Surf Schools
There are lots of surf schools dotted right through the western Algarve. Most of them offer lessons for beginners, improvers and serious surfers, as well as providing accommodation packages and a comprehensive range of hired boards and accessories. Many also offer transport services to where the waves are best that day. If you want better nightlife than the west coast offers, there are several based in Sagres and Lagos, too.

Aljezur
Though there's no beach within walking distance, the charming castle-topped town of Aljezur is handily placed for many of the west's finest surf beaches, including the two waves – an easy beach break and a more notable right-hand point/reef break – offered by Arrifana (p109), the tougher, speedy right-hand point break of shingled Praia do Canal, and the steady lefts and rights of spectacular Praia da Amoreira (p107).

Local Conditions
As the beaches are close together, local surfers tend to keep an eye on conditions and hit several strands in one day. The Algarve's beaches tend to be quite tidal and are usually at their best around high tide. The offshore winds that make for the best surfing are mostly easterlies or northeasterlies, depending on the orientation of the beach.

☑ Top Tips

▶ **Windguru** (www.windguru.com) is worth the effort if you want to know where the waves will be at. Another good resource for beach conditions is the **Hydrographic Institute** (www.hidrografico.pt/qual-e-a-tua-onda.php).

▶ Several hostels and surf schools in the area offer transport to beaches from the region's towns.

▶ Localism isn't a huge problem, but does exist. Be respectful and friendly.

▶ Car crime is prevalent in the Algarve, so don't leave any valuables in the vehicle at beach car parks.

✗ Take a Break

Several of the west coast beaches have one or more bar-restaurants, and many of the region's restaurants open all afternoon to cater for surfers and other beachgoers.

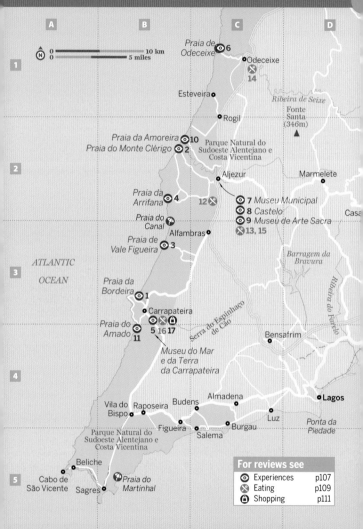

A B C D

1

N
0 _____ 10 km
0 _____ 5 miles

Praia de Odeceixe ◉ **6**

⊗ Odeceixe **14**

Esteveira ●

Ribeira de Seixe

● Rogil

Fonte Santa (346m) ▲

Praia da Amoreira ◉ **10**
Praia do Monte Clérigo ◉ **2**

Parque Natural do Sudoeste Alentejano e Costa Vicentina

● Aljezur

Marmelete ●

2

Praia da Arrifana ◉ **4**

⊗ **12**

◉ **7** *Museu Municipal*
◉ **8** *Castelo*
◉ **9** *Museu de Arte Sacra*
⊗ **13, 15**

Casa

Praia do Canal ⊙

Alfambras ●

Praia de Vale Figueira ◉ **3**

Barragem da Bravura

ATLANTIC

OCEAN

3

Praia da Bordeira ◉ **1**

⊙ Carrapateira ⊙ 🔒

◉ ⊗ ⊙ **5 16 17**

Serra do Espinhaço de Cão

Praia do Amado ◉ **11**

Bensafrim ●

Museu do Mar e da Terra da Carrapateira

4

Vila do Bispo ● Raposeira ●
● Budens
Almadena ●

● **Lagos**

Figueira ●
Salema ●
Burgau ●
Luz ●

Ponta da Piedade

Parque Natural do Sudoeste Alentejano e Costa Vicentina

Beliche ●

5

Cabo de São Vicente ●

Sagres ●

🏛 *Praia do Martinhal*

For reviews see	
◉ Experiences	p107
⊗ Eating	p109
🔒 Shopping	p111

Experiences

Praia da Bordeira & Praia do Amado
BEACH, WALKING

 1, 11 ⊙ Map p106, B3, B4

Carrapateira has two fabulous beaches with spectacular settings and turquoise seas. Bordeira is a mammoth swath of sand merging into dunes 2km from the north side of town. Amado, with even better surf, is at the southern end. The circuit of both from Carrapateira (9km) is a visually stunning hike (or drive), with lookouts over the beaches and the rocky coves and cliffs between them.

Rota Vicentina
HIKING

This long-distance walking route enters the Algarve at Odeceixe and continues right down the west coast to Cabo de São Vicente. The day walk from Odeceixe to Aljezur (18km) is an easy introduction to the trail, heading through mostly flat local farmland. It's a picturesque glimpse of Portuguese rural life. Optional detours take you right to the coast for cliff-top stretches. (www.rotavicentina.com)

Praia da Amoreira
BEACH

 2 ⊙ Map p106, B2

This is the handsomest beach in the Aljezur area, on the north side of the picturesque river mouth and backed by wild dunes. It's 9km by road from Aljezur, signposted off the main road north of town. There's a bar-restaurant here, but no other facilities. You can also access the beach from the southern end (near Praia do Monte Clérigo) if you don't mind getting wet.

Praia de Vale Figueira
BEACH

3 ⊙ Map p106, B3

One of the remoter west coast beaches, this is a wide and magnificent stretch of whitish sand with an ethereal beauty, backed by stratified cliffs hazy in the ocean spray. It's reached by a rough, partly paved road that runs some 5km from the main road at a point 10km north of Carrapateira (take the northern of the two turn-offs). There are no facilities.

Praia da Arrifana
BEACH

4 ⊙ Map p106, B2

This seductive crescent-shaped cove embraced by cliffs, sports an offshore pinnacle and a small fishing harbour. It's wildly popular with surfers of all abilities, has a small beachside restaurant, and clifftop eateries near

☑ Top Tip

Clifftop Views

For a short but spectacular stroll, head to the little village of **Esteveira** (Map p106, C1), near Rogil between Aljezur and Odeceixe. From the tarmac bus turning, head left and a short walk takes you along a river gorge and out to stirring views of the Atlantic. Next stop: East Virginia, USA.

the ruined fortress, which offers breath-taking vistas.

Museu do Mar e da Terra da Carrapateira
MUSEUM

5 Map p106, B3

The Carrapateira Land & Sea Museum is a must for visitors – surfers or otherwise. Up a steep hill near the top of town, its contemporary design space has small exhibits covering everything from the fishing industry to daily life of the locals, and stunning photograph collages depicting Carrapateira of yesteryear (there's minimal English labelling). The vista from the museum's ingenious viewing window over the dunes is sublime. (☏282 970 000; Rua de Pescador, Carrapateira; adult/child €2.70/1.10; ⏰10am-5pm Tue-Sat)

Praia de Odeceixe
BEACH

6 Map p106, C1

This tongue of sand is winningly set at a river mouth and flanked by imposing schist cliffs. It's a good family option, as smaller kids can paddle on the peaceful river side of the strand. It's 3.5km from the endearing whitewashed village of Odeceixe, a hub of budget accommodation. The beach itself has eating, sleeping and surfing options.

Odeceixe Surf School
SURFING

This friendly set-up offers surfing classes (and board and wetsuit rental), with sites both on and just above Praia de Odeceixe (see 6 Map p106, C1); look for the octopus sign. It'll transport you to whatever local beach has the best waves that day and can arrange packages with accommodation. (☏963 170 493; www.odeceixesurfschool.com; Praia de Odeceixe; 1-/3-/5-day courses €55/150/225; ⏰10.30am-7pm)

Arrifana Surf School
SURFING

Offers a complete range of hire and lessons, as well as packages with accommodation on offer at Praia da Arrifana (see 4 Map p106, B2). (☏917 862 138; www.arrifanasurfschool.com; Praia da Arrifana; 1-/3-/4-/5-day course €55/150/200/225; ⏰Mar-Oct)

Amado Surfcamp
SURFING

Just above Praia do Amado (see 11 Map p106, B4), Amado Surfcamp offers various packages in different kinds of accommodation, and also does private classes and day courses. (☏927 831 568; www.amadosurfcamp.com; 1-week package incl accommodation, breakfast, equipment hire & lessons €425-525, camping €325)

Algarve Surf School
SURFING

Based at Praia do Amado (see 11 Map p106, B4), these guys offer classes for all abilities and packages including hostel accommodation in Sagres or Lagos, meals and transfers. Kids' lessons also available. (☏962 846 771; www.algarvesurf-school.com; Praia do Amado; day lesson €55)

Museu Municipal MUSEUM

7 Map p106, C2

This small but likeable museum has three rooms. Downstairs is an archaeological collection displaying everything from Stone Age axes to a 16th-century whipping post, while across the hall the Islamic section has a good selection of locally produced ceramics. Upstairs is an ethnographic display with everything from clocks to carts. Info is in Portuguese. An English video explains the area's attractions, which include three nearby museums that you can enter on the same ticket. (Largo 5 de Outubro, Aljezur; entry to 4 museums €2; 9am-1pm & 2-6pm Tue-Sat)

Castelo CASTLE

8 Map p106, C2

The polygonal castle, on the site of an Iron Age fort, was built by the Moors in the 10th century, conquered by the Christians in 1249, then abandoned in the late 15th century. The walls and a couple of towers survive, as well as a cistern. Great views of the surrounding area can be had from the rock in the middle of the fortress. (Aljezur; admission free; 24hr)

Museu de Arte Sacra MUSEUM

9 Map p106, C2

Built in the 16th century and damaged in the 1755 earthquake, the modest Igreja da Misericórdia church was reconstructed in the 18th century. Its small religious-art museum houses items

donated by a locally born Monsignor. The highlights are the old church bell and a 14th-century crown. Visit the museum first, and the guardian will open the church for you. (Rua do Castelo, Aljezur; entry to 4 museums €2; 9am-1pm & 2-6pm Tue-Sat)

Praia do Monte Clérigo BEACH

10 Map p106, B2

One of the emblematic beaches southwest of Aljezur, Monte Clérigo is a deep strip of sand with a fairly sedate atmosphere. Behind it is a small village with plenty of holiday rental houses.

Eating

Gulli ITALIAN €€

12 Map p106, C2

On the main road 4km south of Aljezur, this looks like a standard driver's lunch stop until you enter and discover

✅ Top Tip

Cheap Sleeps

Odeceixe (Map p106, C1) has several cheap places to stay and private homes offering *quartos* (rooms) on its small network of central streets.

a handsome modern interior and a menu of not just pizzas, but rather innovative, quality Med mains using excellent ingredients. There are various degustation options, so kick back, order some wine, designate a driver and enjoy. (📞282 994 344; Sítio de Santa Susana, N120; mains €11-18; ⊙12.30pm-midnight Tue-Sun)

Pont'a Pé

PORTUGUESE €€

13 🍴 Map p106, C3

With wooden floors and a beamed ceiling, this friendly place does tasty dishes with a range of different fish, and good barbecue chicken. The daily specials are always delicious and interesting. (📞282 998 104; www.pontape.pt; Largo da Liberdade 12, Aljezur; mains €8-12; ⊙10am-11pm Mon-Sat)

Sítio do Rio

SEAFOOD €€

Right on the dunes near Praia da Bordeira (see 1 ◉ Map p106, B3), this good-value restaurant cooks up excellent grilled fish and meat mains; there are also vegetarian choices. It has an appealing indoor area, with fishing nets on the walls, and outdoor seating under large umbrellas. It's hugely popular at weekends. (📞282 973 119; Estrada da Praia da Bordeira, Carrapateira; mains €9-15; ⊙lunch & dinner Wed-Mon; 🛜🖊)

O Paulo

SEAFOOD €€

Spectacularly set by the ruined fortress of Arrifana (see 4 ◉ Map p106, B2), with majestic cliff-top views as far as Cabo São Vicente, O Paulo has a covered terrace that makes a romantic spot for a meal. The vistas are hard to live up to, but it does a pretty good job here, with plates – just about all seafood – full of flavour and colour. (📞282 995 184; www.restauranteopaulo.com; Arrifana; mains €12-20; ⊙9.30am-10pm; 🛜)

Taberna do Gabão

PORTUGUESE €€

14 🍴 Map p106, C1

Odeceixe's best option, this welcoming restaurant features good-value traditional dishes served in a charming old-fashioned wooden dining room. There's a small patio for outdoor seating. (📞282 947 549; Rua do Gabão 9, Odeceixe; mains €7-13; ⊙lunch & dinner Wed-Mon)

Restaurante Ruth o Ivo

SEAFOOD €€

15 🍴 Map p106, C3

This is a casual nautical-themed eatery, often recommended by locals for its seafood dishes and honest fare. Look out for *perceves* (goose barnacles) if it has them: it's a local speciality with a memorably marine, if acquired, taste. (📞282 998 534; Rua 25 de Abril 14, Aljezur; mains €9-16; ⊙lunch & dinner)

Traditional *cataplana* (seafood stew; p47)

Sítio do Forno　　　SEAFOOD €€

On the cliff overlooking Praia do Amado in Carrapateira (see 11 ⊙ Map p106, B4), this large place grew from a tiny fisherman's cabana. The value is in the setting (with its magnificent ocean views), not so much in the cuisine (though some fish dishes are delicious, depending on what's available). (☏282 973 914; mains €10-17; ⊘noon-10pm Tue-Sun Jan-Nov; 🛜)

Microbar Carrapateira　CAFE €

16 ✖ Map p106, B3

The name certainly conceals just how much this excellent place on the square has to offer. Whatever you feel like, it's got it. That includes surfer comfort food, including tasty bruschetta, generous hamburgers and vegetarian options; an ice-cold *imperial* (small draught beer); moist cakes; soy coffee; or a cocktail in the sun. (Largo do Comercio, Carrapateira; meals €5-10; ⊘10am-10pm)

Shopping

Mercado Municipal　　MARKET

17 🔒 Map p106, B3

Located near the bridge in Carrapateira, the municipal market is a good place to buy fresh fruit and vegies, and has a very appealing fish counter. (⊘8am-2pm Mon-Sat)

The Best of
the Algarve

The Algarve's Best...

Benagil beach, accessed by Percurso dos
Sete Vales Suspensos (p66)
WESTEND61/GETTY IMAGES ©

Best
Beaches

The coast of the Algarve is a seemingly endless series of some of the continent's finest beaches. The climate and atmosphere feel Mediterranean, but this is the Atlantic, so good waves and first-rate water sports are available alongside more sedate family-oriented paddling zones. With more than 150 beaches, this is one of Europe's capitals of sun, sand and surf.

ANUNES PHOTO/GETTY IMAGES ©

Options Galore

There are so many superb beaches in the Algarve that any attempt to list the best is, in a sense, doomed to failure. You're sure to find your own favourite that doesn't feature here. One of the region's appealing features is that there's such a variety of conditions in a relatively small area, so you're never far away from some safe toddler paddle play, a legendary point break or a calm stretch of water for a bit of breaststroke.

West Coast Beaches

The west coast is particularly good for surfing, with a series of west- and southwest-facing beaches that see some big swells. They are divided by sharp schist headlands that provide some excellent point breaks when conditions are right.

South Coast Beaches

The south coast in general has softer waves, with a series of picturesque beaches backed by sculptured limestone formations in the western half of the region. The eastern segment has a series of evocative island beaches that are the outer section of the complex of dunes and lagoons that forms the Parque Natural da Ria Formosa. Accessed by boat, they are romantic spots.

Best Remote Beaches

Praia de Vale Figueira Lonely, lovely stretch of sea spray and sand at the end of a long byroad. (p107)

Praia do Barril On Ilha de Tavira, atmospheric former tuna-fishing settlement now reached by a little train or a dune boardwalk. (p45)

Praia de Cacela Velha Opposite the jewel-like village of the same name, this is a hard-to-get-to beach with a summer LGBTIQ scene. (p41)

Ilha da Armona Part of the Parque Natural da Ria Formosa this island offers remote, deserted sands and a busier family-oriented strip. (p27)

Ilha de Tavira Large sandy island with an excellent beach opposite

Praia do Amado (p107)

Tavira, and long lonely strands to explore. (p45)

Best Family Beaches

Praia de Odeceixe Tongue of sand with kid-friendly river side and livelier ocean breakers. (p108; pictured left)

Praia Fluvial de Alcoutim Not to be outdone by the coast, this inland town has created a tiny beach resort on a quiet river bend. (p43)

Praia do Martinhal By the charming town of Sagres, this is a postcard pretty beach. (p97)

Praia do Carvoeiro This tiny but likeable beach is the focus of the well-kept resort town of Carvoeiro. (p66)

Best Surf Beaches

Praia da Arrifana Classic surf beach with a beach break and a point break; also family friendly. (p107)

Praia da Bordeira & Praia do Amado The twin beaches of Carrapateira offer good surf and picturesque coastal scenery. (p107; pictured above)

Praia da Amoreira Spectacular stretch at a river mouth backed by rolling wild dunes. (p107)

Praia do Monte Clérigo Deep swath of sand backed by a small hamlet of holiday rentals. (p109)

Best Strollable Beaches

Praia da Falésia Long handsome beach backed by cliffs of many differ-

ent shades of ochre and white. (p55)

Praia da Marinha A stunning ensemble of sculpted limestone makes this one of the region's most photogenic beaches. (p66)

Meia Praia Gorgeous beach stretching into the distance from the party town of Lagos. (p81)

Praia da Rocha Touristy but magnificent, this wide, wide strand keeps all comers happy. (p63)

Praia da Galé Long, upmarket sandy strand to the west of Albufeira with plenty of room to move. (p56)

Best
Dining

Best Views

O Luar da Fóia Just outside Monchique; an excellent rustic restaurant with a view. (p76)

A Fábrica do Costa Seafood in a stunning setting right on the water near Cacela Velha. (p41)

F Restaurante Delicious seafood and polite service overlooking the beach in Praia da Rocha. (p63)

Best Vegetarian

Mum's A postsurf sensation; serves delicious vegetarian and seafood dishes. (p98)

Gengibre e Canela One of the Algarve's best vegetarian restaurants in the centre of Faro. (p34)

Best Rural

Veneza One of our favourite rural restaurants in the Algarve; well worth seeking out. (p57)

Restaurante O Barradas Stunning fare just outside of Silves. (p67)

Monte da Eira Country restaurant offering high-class food in a converted mill. (p57)

Best Traditional

A Casínha Try traditional Portuguese dishes at this smart Sagres eatery. (p98)

A Charrete Try typical Algarve hill cuisine in this atmospheric, old-fashioned spot in Monchique. (p76)

Faz Gostos In Faro's old town; presents excellent French-influenced fare. (p33)

Pont'a Pé Reliably excellent family-run place serving great fish to hungry surfers. (p110)

Best Innovative

Vila Joya Near Albufeira; often regarded as Portugal's best fine-dining restaurant. (p57)

Gulli Italian-influenced gastronomic treat; a real roadside surprise. (p109)

Tacho à Mesa The freshest of market produce in this luminous modern restaurant in Olhão. (p29)

MATT MUNRO / LONELY PLANET ©

Best No-Frills

Chefe Branco Typical Portuguese neighbourhood restaurant; simple, friendly and great. (p34)

Casinha do Petisco It's usually a struggle to get a table at this loveable Lagos eatery, it's so popular. (p85)

Casa A. Corvo A cheap-looking terrace, a barbecue, and the freshest of fish at great prices in Fuzeta. (p27)

Casa Simão Zero romance, but delicious family-cooked Portuguese food in Tavira. (p46)

A Forja Top-quality traditional food in Lagos at great prices. (p85)

Best
Historic
Architecture

Best Churches

Igreja de São Lourenço de Matos The blue-and-white-tiled interior of this small roadside church makes it one of the most stunning sights in the Algarve. (p55)

Sé de Faro The centrepiece of Faro's old town offers a museum and super views from its bell tower. (p24)

Igreja de Nossa Senhora do Carmo This Faro church is most notable for its spooky chapel built of skulls and bones. (p31)

Igreja de Santo António Accessed through the municipal museum in Lagos, this is a baroque and roll extravaganza. (p83)

Nossa Senhora da Conceição This chapel in Loulé has an undistinguished exterior, but a vibrant baroque interior. (p55)

Igreja Matriz de Monchique Hill-town church with several typically offbeat Manueline architectural features. (p75)

Sé de Silves The best-preserved Gothic church in the Algarve has a high, simple and typically elegant interior. (p65; pictured right)

Museu de Arte Sacra Superbly restored 18th-century chapel in Albufeira with a collection of religious art from the surrounding region. (p56)

Best Castles & Fortresses

Fortaleza de Sagres Stern bastions guard an open expanse of cliff top with extensive coastal views. (p92)

Castelo de Silves The restored walls of this Moorish-era castle offer commanding vistas over this atmospheric town. (p65)

Castelo de Castro Marim The Algarve's most impressive medieval fortress stretches over a large area and has a very authentic ambience. (p43)

Castelo de Tavira The shell of the walls of this

GTW/GETTY IMAGES ©

formerly formidable castle house a peaceful botanic garden. (p46)

Castelo de Alcoutim Overlooking the Guadiana in the northeast Algarve, this atmospheric castle contains a good museum. (p42)

Castelo de Aljezur Top of the town in this popular base for surfers, this fortress is bare but atmospheric. (p109)

Fortaleza da Ponta da Bandeira As fortresses go, this is in the chihuahua class, but makes an interesting visit on the Lagos waterfront. (p83)

Best
Birdwatching

The Algarve is an increasingly popular destination for birdwatching. Its geographical position makes it an important stopover for migratory birds, while the quantity of wetland environments offers an ideal habitat for waders and ducks. Offshore are numerous species of seabirds, including several that are rare in the rest of Europe.

Sagres The area around the southwest corner of Portugal is particularly noteworthy during the autumn migration season, as hundreds of raptors pass overhead on their way to their African wintering. The area is also good year-round for seabird watching. (p90)

Reserva Natural do Sapal de Castro Marim This 20-sq-km stretch of marshland and salt pans bordering the Rio Guadiana is an excellent birdwatching spot. Important winter visitors include greater flamingos, spoonbills and Caspian terns. In spring it's busy with white storks. Park headquarters is 2km east of the N122, 1.5km north of Castro Marim. Cerro do Bufo, 2km southwest of Castro Marim, is another rewarding birding area. (p43)

Parque Natural da Ria Formosa This coastal park of tidal estuaries and dune islands makes an ideal waterbird habitat, with over 20,000 birds, particularly ducks and waders, using this as their wintering grounds. Iconic species include the purple gallinule and hard-to-spot little bittern. Specialised birdwatching boat trips leave from several of the towns in the area. (p26)

Lagoa dos Salgados Between the resorts of Albufeira and Armação de Pêra, this shallow marshy lagoon is a popular place to watch waders, including flamingos, spoonbills and the purple gallinule, with rare species frequently sighted. There's also a large number and variety of duck species.

☑ Top Tips

▶ **Algarve Tourism** (www.visitalgarve.pt) produces a guide to birdwatching in the region, available from tourist offices (€7) or downloadable from its website.

▶ **Birds and Nature** (☎913 299 990; www.birds.pt) is one of Portugal's best established birdwatching set-ups, with various day and multiday tours in the Algarve.

▶ **Simon Wates** (☎282 639 418; www.algarvebirdman.com) is a recommended birdwatching guide with a deep knowledge of the region.

▶ See p127 for recommended birdwatching boat trips.

Best
Festivals

Carnaval de Loulé (www.cm-loule.pt) There are Carnaval celebrations all across the region, but Loulé's is the biggest, boldest and sexiest. There's a kids' parade on the Friday preceding Shrove Tuesday, and the main event on Sunday, in February or early March.

Feira dos Enchidos Tradicionais (www.cm-monchique.pt) This lively March sausage festival in Monchique showcases the best of traditional mountain cured meats.

Fiesa (www.fiesa.org) On the beach at Armação de Pêra; a high-quality sand-sculpture contest that's there for the whole of the season (mid-March to mid-October), with a different theme each year.

FestivalMed (www.festivalmed.pt) Held in late June in Loulé; has fast gained a reputation as a quality world-music festival.

Feira da Serra (http://feiradaserra.cm-sbras.pt) Down-home country fair held in late July in São Brás de Aportel; boasts locally produced goodies and has plenty of folkloric song and dance performances.

Festival do Marisco (www.festivaldomarisco.com) In Olhão, this seafood extravaganza in August is a huge knees-up.

Feira Medieval de Silves (www.cm-silves.pt) Held over nine days in August, the medieval past of Silves comes to life with food stalls, costumes and events.

Festival da Sardinha (www.festivaldasardinha.pt) In August the fishing town of Portimão celebrates Portugal's favourite fish, the sardine, with associated music, dance and festivities.

FolkFaro (www.folkfaro.com) Faro's big folk festival features lots of dance (with local and international folk groups), live music and street fests. It's held over a week in late August at various venues around town.

JULIOC/GETTY IMAGES ©

☑ **Top Tip**

▶ Even the smallest village will have a yearly festival with music, dancing, a funfair and food stalls. These are especially common between June and September, so if you're in the Algarve at this time, you're likely to be able to find one of these local celebrations.

Feira de Santa Iria (www.cm-faro.pt) In late October Faro's biggest traditional event honours St Irene with fairground rides, stalls and entertainment. It takes place in a temporary fairground to the northeast.

Best
Nightlife

Best Local Spots

Poeta Caffe This sweet little spot in Loulé has a lovely patio and a friendly, inclusive vibe. (p58)

Nana's Bar In Praia da Rocha; has a far more local scene than the downmarket tourist traps on the waterfront. Good drinks and a cheery Portuguese atmosphere. (p63)

Barlefante Tucked away in a narrow Monchique alley, this is an enticing hideaway. (p77)

Taberna dos Frades A great local vibe in this welcoming Loulé bar, which is a venue for anything from tapas to fado. (p58)

Best Setting

O Castelo Marvellous views over the water from Faro's old town; regular events. (p37)

Restaurante Boneca Bar Cutely tucked into rocks on the beach, this is a memorable sunset spot at Carvoeiro. (p69)

Duna Beach Club Right on Meia Praia beach by Lagos, this is a sandside hang-out by day and upmarket cocktail spot by night. (p88)

Best Mixed Drinks

Columbus Bar Faro's best bar mixes superlative drinks and has a great mix of people in its handsome interior, as well as grab-'em-if-you-can outdoor tables. (p37)

Tavira Lounge By the river in Tavira; seamlessly converts itself from a cafe by day to a cocktail lounge-bar by night. (p49)

Taberna de Lagos More upmarket that many in Lagos, this stylish bar in a historic building mixes a great gin and tonic. (p88)

Best Postsurf

Bon Vivant One of Lagos' best all-round choices, with a roof terrace, upbeat bar staff and excellent cocktails. (p87)

PETER ADAMS/GETTY IMAGES ©

☑ **Top Tip**

▶ While in more touristy zones, many bars will open in the afternoon or early evening, in other places don't be surprised if a bar doesn't open its doors until 10pm or 11pm, closing at 2am or 4am.

Agua Salgada One of the liveliest of a strip of surfer-oriented cafe-restaurant-bars in lovely little Sagres. At night DJs ensure it's party time. (p100)

Warung A great postsurf choice in Sagres, with a laid-back atmosphere and friendly scene. (p100)

Best
Cafes

Portugal has famously delicious and inexpensive coffee, a legacy of its imperial days. A popular venue for a morning or afternoon caffeine stop is the *pastelaria,* a local cake-and-pastry shop that serves coffee, tea, herbal infusions and sometimes light meals.

Gardy One of Faro's classic cafes, as much a spot for people-watching on the pedestrian street as a place for delicious pastries. (p35)

Maktostas Downbeat and bohemian Faro venue for beer, coffee and toasted sandwiches. A top spot. (p34)

Café Gombá Long a Lagos favourite for mid-morning or midafternoon pastries. (p86)

Mimar Café Excellent all-round choice in Lagos, good at any time of the day. (p86)

Café Calcinha Historic Loulé cafe that doesn't seem to have changed too much in its near-century of existence. (p58)

Ó Chá Lá Friendly tea house tucked away in the higher part of the likeable hill village of Monchique. (p76)

Microbar Carrapateira Little more than a kiosk, this surf-village spot manages to service its outdoor tables with everything from meals to cocktails. (p111)

A Casa da Isabel Housed in a beautiful Portimão mansion; a great stop for a range of teas and pastries. (p62)

Agua Mel Top choice for snacks, delicious cakes and coffee with a view in the hill town of Alte. (p53)

Café Inglês Lovely outdoor seating, live music, great food, desserts and drinks in Silves. (p67)

Pastelaria Rosa Historic tiled cafe with lots of enchantment in Silves. (p67)

VIENNETTA/GETTY IMAGES ©

☑ Top Tip

▶ There's a great selection of sweet offerings in the region's cafes, including the Algarve's famous range of marzipan sweets, as well as the classic Portuguese *pastéis de nata,* iconic custard tarts seen everywhere and best eaten warm and dusted with cinnamon.

Pastelaria Tavirense This could almost define the *pastelaria* genre and is the social heart of Tavira. (p48)

Best
For Families

It's hard to envisage a destination that is better set up for kids than the Algarve, and it's a deservedly popular family-holiday spot. Apart from the great weather and the dozens of child-friendly beaches, there's a plethora of family activities on offer, from zoos and water parks to boat trips, horse riding and more.

UNCLEWIL.COM/GETTY IMAGES ©

Algarve Advantages

One of the big advantages of the Algarve as a family destination is the short travel times between attractions, minimising the risk of kids getting frazzled by long car trips. Children are very welcome everywhere, and lots of restaurants have a children's section of the menu.

Forward Planning

Though the region is chock-full of family attractions, a bit of preplanning is rewarding. There are many water parks, but children under five aren't allowed on most rides, so if you've got a range of ages, it might be wise to choose a park that has alternative attractions such as animals. Queues for rides can be long in July and August, but visiting midweek can help. Food and beverages are expensive and, while bringing your own is often technically not permitted, checks are rare.

Family Accommodation

Accommodation is easy, with numerous apartments offering kitchen facilities and flexible sleeping arrangements. Even in hotels and B&Bs, most choices will put a cot or extra bed into a room for a small extra charge. Read the fine print though, as there are increasing numbers of boutique or resort-style hotels that don't accept younger children.

☑ Top Tips

▶ For most of the big-ticket attractions, particularly for water parks, you can save substantial amounts of cash, as well as queuing time, by prepurchasing tickets online.

▶ Most car-hire companies offer child seats, but it's worth booking these well in advance if you can, as numbers are usually limited.

Best Water Parks

Slide & Splash Portugal's best water park will keep kids and adults entertained for hours with its huge range of aquatic attractions. (p66)

Dolphins

Aquashow This is a massive complex with a whole range of water-park attractions plus roller coasters and an on-site hotel. (p56)

Aqualand Yet another excellent water park offering a variety of attractions, among which the huge loop-the-loop slide has the biggest wow factor. (p57)

Krazy World Water park and crocodiles, appropriately separated, plus plenty more. (p65)

Best Boat Trips

Mar Ilimitado Ecologically sound dolphin-

and birdwatching trips operating out of Sagres. (p97)

Formosamar Great boat trips around the estuaries and islands near Faro. (p31)

Algarve Dolphins This set-up offers excellent dolphin-watching trips running from Lagos. (p83)

Best Water Sports

Lands Try some sea kayaking in the calm waters off Faro. (p27)

Algarve Surf School This set-up runs parallel lessons for kids, so the

whole family can learn at the same time. (p108)

Best Animal Experiences

Parque Zoológico de Lagos This popular zoo west of Lagos has lots of primates and a zone of gentle pettable farm animals. (p84)

Burros e Artes Offers multiday donkey treks, as well as shorter excursions suitable for younger children. (p109)

Albufeira Riding Centre Recommended horse-riding set-up; good with kids of all ages. (p56)

Best
Golf

With benevolent weather and some 50 courses in a relatively small area, the Algarve is one of Europe's top golfing destinations. High-end courses with big-name designers and state-of-the-art landscaping predominate, though there are also some humbler, cheaper options.

STEVE PHOTOGRAPHY/SHUTTERSTOCK ©

Monte Rei (✆281 950 950; www.monte-rei.com; Sesmarias, Vila Nova da Cacela) This Jack Nicklaus–designed course northeast of Tavira is the Algarve's most handsome – and among its most expensive at about €200 a round. It's visually stunning, with challenging holes, lots of water and elegantly sculpted bunkers.

Oceânico (✆289 310 333; www.oceanicogolf.com; Volta do Medronheiro, Vilamoura) At the sprawling Vilamoura resort, this enormous complex offers five high-standard courses, as well as a couple of others in other parts of the Algarve.

Penina (✆282 420 200; www.penina.com; 2 players plus buggy €195) Between Lagos and Portimão, this is the original Algarve golf course and, for a championship course, offers comparatively affordable green fees.

Pestana (www.pestanagolf. com) This hotel group runs several courses, which are among the Algarve's more inexpensive rounds – mostly in the order of €40 to €60 a game. Several are near Carvoeiro.

San Lorenzo (✆289 396 522; www.sanlorenzogolf course.com; Vale do Lobo; green fees €110-140) Just west of Faro, this is one of the Algarve's premier courses, with a world-class oceanside layout.

☑Top Tips

▸ Club hire is available at **Aeroporto de Faro** (FAO; ✆289 800 800; www.ana.pt; 📶); book your set at www.clubstohire. com.

▸ The website www. algarvegolf.net offers discounted green-fee reservation at many of the Algarve's courses.

▸ Look for packages including flights, accommodation and green fees for the most affordable golf trips.

Best
Markets

Portugal is still a country where markets are an important part of commerce and play a big role in society. The Algarve has plenty of interesting ones to visit. Marvelling at the fresh fish in the municipal food markets is always a delight, while rotating village markets combine cheap tat with authentic locally produced items.

DAVID HANSON/GETTY IMAGES ©

Municipal Markets

In many ways the best and most authentic markets are the municipal covered markets found in most towns. These open Monday to Saturday mornings and are great for a stroll to examine the fresh fruit and vegetables, and fish and meat counters. It's the best option for self-caterers, and the most sustainable way to shop for food in the Algarve. In fishing towns, the *lota* is where the fresh fish off the boats is auctioned to restaurants and fishmongers; not a place to make purchases yourself, but often an interesting spectacle.

Other Algarve Markets

Other markets occur weekly, fortnightly or monthly on different days. These tend to combine local specialities – warm woollens, brassware and Moorish-influenced ceramics, for example – with low-quality sweatshop-produced underwear and other cut-price clothing. Still, they are always worth a wander, and you can find some good bargains. Some of them have secondhand stalls, too.

São Brás de Alportel (⊘8am–1pm) Held every Saturday morning, this is a market with a bit of everything.

Loulé (⊘8am-2pm) The Saturday-morning market here is famous and attracts plenty of tourists, but also has plenty of worthless tat.

Lagos (⊘8am–2pm) An all-purpose market is held at the bus station every Saturday morning.

Faro (⊘7.30am–2pm) A flea market is held in the stadium car park on the first and third Sunday of every month.

Monchique (⊘8am–2pm) On the second Friday of every month, there's a handicrafts and clothes market with food stalls.

Best
Museums

Museu Municipal de Arqueologia Albufeira's museum of local finds is a welcome counterpoint to its tacky tourist pubs. (p55)

Museu Municipal, Aljezur Interesting displays on ethnography and the Moorish era, plus access to other museums around town. (p109)

Pólo Museológico de Salir Small display in what's left of Salir's castle. (p53)

Museu do Mar e da Terra da Carrapateira Atop the surf village of Carrapateira is an excellent display on maritime and local life. (p108)

Museu Municipal, Faro One of the Algarve's best archaeological museums, with high-quality pieces from different periods housed in a beautiful building. (p31)

Museu Municipal, Lagos An astonishingly varied collection, this museum will have something for everyone. (p83; pictured right)

Museu Municipal, Loulé Occupying the town's castle; has an interesting and wide-ranging display. (p55)

Museu de Portimão This brilliant former tuna cannery gives all the details about the industry and more. (p63)

Museu dos Faróis Small but perfectly formed, this little museum at the end of Portugal covers navigation and lighthouses. (p95)

Museu Municipal de Arqueologia This museum in Silves includes a fabulous in-situ Moorish well and parts of the town walls. (p65)

Museu Etnográfico do Trajo Algarvio A

PAUL BERNHARDT/GETTY IMAGES ©

☑ **Top Tip**

▶ Most of the Algarve's museums are on the small side: good to bear in mind when budgeting your time.

recommended spot that presents traditional costumes and info on the cork industry. (p59)

Núcleo Islâmico Tavira's most interesting museum focuses on the town's Islamic past. (p45)

Best
Water Activities

WESTEND61/GETTY IMAGES ©

For such a coastal destination, it's no surprise that what you can do on or under the water is basically only limited by the time you have available. There are numerous operators offering boat trips of all types, or take to the ocean yourself with a surfboard, scuba tank, sea kayak or kite rig.

Best Boat Trips & Wildlife-Watching

Formosamar Excellent wildlife-spotting boat trips around the Ria Formosa park. (p31)

Natura Algarve Dolphin- and bird-spotting trips around the eastern Algarve. (p31)

Algarve Dolphins Reliable and responsible dolphin-watching in Lagos. (p83)

Dolphins Driven Dolphin-watching excursions and coastal explorations from Albufeira. (p56)

Riverwatch Birdwatching tours to a small wetland area north of Lagos. (p84)

Mar Ilimitado Excellent, environmentally focused dolphin- and birdwatching trips out of Sagres. (p97)

Passeios Ria Formosa Various boat trips to explore the estuaries and islands of the park. (p45)

Best Diving

Divers Cove Multilingual centre offering hire, dives and Professional Association of Diving Instructors (PADI) courses. (p66)

Blue Ocean Reliable centre with a full offering of courses, dives and hire. (p83)

DiversCape Based at the harbour in Sagres; competent, recommended diving operator. (p97)

Best Kayaking

Lands Reliable set-up offering kayak hire and tours; based in Faro. (p27)

Axessextreme Sea-kayaking excursions in the western Algarve. (p84)

Best Surfing & More

Arrifana Surf School A complete range of hire and lessons. (p108)

Algarve Surf School Based at Praia do Amado, but offer transfers from other towns. (p108)

Odeceixe Surf School Friendly set-up based at Odeceixe beach on the west coast. (p108)

Lagos Surf Center Surf classes with family options available. (p84)

Windsurf Point At Meia Praia by Lagos; all you need to get out on a sailboard. (p84)

Sagres Natura One of the best of several Sagres-based surf schools. (p97)

Kitesurf Eolis Excellent kiting operator based east of Tavira. (p46)

Best
Outdoors

The Algarve's attractions aren't limited to water. The beautifully rural interior, with its rolling hills, is great walking country, and there are some top day walks as well as long-distance routes crossing the region. There are also lots of horse-riding centres, as well as mountain biking and more.

WESTEND61/GETTY IMAGES ©

Best Walking

Via Algarviana This long-distance walk crosses the region; some of its stages make great day walks. (p72)

Rota Vicentina Tramp down the Algarve's west coast. (p107)

Percurso dos Sete Vales Suspensos Spectacular cliff-top walk between glorious beaches. (p66)

Rocha da Pena Classic hill walk of the Serra do Caldeirão region. (p53)

Fóia It's a lovely hike from Monchique up to this, the Algarve's highest point. (p75)

Walkin'Sagres Great walking excursions around Sagres. (p97)

Burros e Artes Multiday treks across the Algarve with donkeys carrying the gear. (p109)

Best Biking

Mountain Bike Adventure Full range of excursions, from gentle downhills to technical black routes. (p85)

Alternativtour Mountain-biking tours, as well as guided walks, canoeing and more. (p76)

Outdoor Tours Good biking and walking excursions. (p75)

Best Horse Riding

Albufeira Riding Centre Good range of rides for

☑ **Top Tip**

▶ Head to the **Termas de Monchique Spa** (☎282 910 910; www.monchique termas.com; admission €15, hotel guests €12; ⏱mid-Feb–Dec) for a well-deserved soak after walking the nearby hills.

all abilities and well-cared-for horses. (p56)

Tiffany's Based near Lagos; offers various horse-riding excursions. (p84)

Country Riding Centre Rides for all levels in the Silves countryside. (p66)

Survival Guide

Survival Guide

Before You Go

When to Go (Lagos)

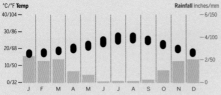

°C/°F Temp
40/104 —
30/86 —
20/68 —
10/50 —
0/32 —

Rainfall inches/mm
— 6/150
— 4/100
— 2/50
— 0

J F M A M J J A S O N D

➡ **Spring (Mar–May)**
Admire almond and orange blossoms, and hike inland amid wildflowers.

➡ **Summer (Jun–Aug)**
High temperatures and accommodation prices, crowded beaches and pumping nightlife. June is notably quieter.

➡ **Autumn (Sep–Nov)**
The sea is still warm enough for swimming, but the crowds have dropped off. Great time to visit.

➡ **Winter (Dec–Feb)**
Low prices but mild temperatures and still plenty of sunshine.

Book Your Stay

☑ **Top Tip** Book accommodation well in advance if you'll be visiting in the July–August high season.

➡ Accommodation prices are at their highest in the summer season, with top rates charged from mid-July to the end of August. Many places demand a minimum stay at this time, usually two or three days, but sometimes up to a week.

➡ Conversely, shoulder- and low-season prices can be heavily discounted, offering great value.

➡ Especially on the coast in summer, you can often rent a *quarto* (room) in a private house. These usually have a shared bathroom and are cheap and spotless. If you're not approached by an owner (often sturdy old ladies) or don't spot a sign (*se aluga quarto*), ask at the local tourist office for a list.

➡ There are numerous rental houses and apartments in the Algarve; start your search with **Airbnb** (www.airbnb.com) or **House Trip** (www.housetrip.com).

➡ Budget accommodation ranges from the hostel (*hostel* or *pousada de juventude*) to the *residencial*, *casa de hóspedes*, *pensão* and *hospedaria*, which are various types of guesthouse.

➡ Campsites are ubiquitous along the coast,

anging from cheap
municipal spots to well-
equipped parks run by
Orbitur (www.orbitur.pt).

Useful Websites

Booking.com (www.
booking.com) Compre-
hensive online hotel- and
apartment-booking
service, with a handy
app for reservations on
the hoof.

Lonely Planet (www.
lonelyplanet.com) Travellers'
forum, author reviews and
recommendations, plus
online booking.

Pousadas (www.pousadas.
pt) Network of luxurious
government-run historic
hotels.

Visit Algarve (www.
visitalgarve.pt) The tourist-
board website has useful
accommodation listings
by category.

Best Budget

Casa d'Alagoa (www.
farohostel.com) Handsome,
friendly and central hostel
in Faro.

**Pousada de Juventude
Tavira** (www.pousadas
juventude.pt) One of Portugal's best official hostels.

Quinta do Coração (www.
algarveparadise.com) Lovely
hill-country setting and a

range of rustic
accommodation.

Amazigh Hostel (www.
amazighostel.com) Laid-back
surfer hang-out perfect for
the west coast beaches.

**Pousada de Juventude
Lagos** (www.pousadas
juventude.pt) Well-equipped
and in the heart of the
Lagos nightlife zone.

Pensão Bicuar (www.
pensionbicuar.com) A range
of characterful accommo-
dation in Olhão's centre.

Best Midrange

Casa Beleza do Sul
(www.casabelezadosul.com)
Gloriously characterful
apartments in historic
Tavira building.

B&B Candelária (www.
casa-candelaria.com) En-
chanting, rustic spot in a
quiet hill village.

O Castelo (www.ocastelo.
net) Sparkling and warmly
welcoming choice above
Carvoeiro's petite beach.

Tavira Inn (www.tavira-inn.
com) Offbeat riverside
guesthouse with lots of
quirky charm.

Inn Seventies (www.inn
seventies.com) Sumptuous
retro suites in the heart of
Lagos.

Casa Azul (www.casaazul
sagres.com) Cheerful, top-
value, surfer-friendly hotel
in Sagres.

Best Top End

Quinta da Lua (www.
quintadalua.com.pt) Super
boutique retreat in the
countryside near Tavira.

**Pousada do Palácio
de Estoi** (www.pousadas.
pt) Sumptuous palace
near Faro, with rooms in a
modern wing.

Hotel da Rocha (www.
hoteldarocha.com) Stylish
and smart modern rooms
by the beach in Praia da
Rocha.

Vila Joya (www.vilajoya.
com) Ultraluxurious resort
near Albufeira for ultimate
Algarve pampering.

Casa Vicentina (www.
casavicentina.pt) Secluded
and chic rural retreat on
the west coast.

Vila São Vicente (www.
hotelsaovicentealbufeira.
com) Classy, well-run hotel
right above the beach in
Albufeira.

Arriving in
the Algarve

☑ **Top Tip** Shuttle
services based at **Faro**

Airport (FAO; 📞 289 800 800; www.ana.pt; 📶) can zip you anywhere in the Algarve cheaper than a taxi. It's best to prebook.

From Faro Airport

➡ **Próximo** (www.proximo.pt; €2.22, 20 minutes) bus number 14 runs infrequently to central Faro, while the more regular number 16 runs to Faro's bus station via the train station hourly or better, from 5.20am to 11.20pm. In the other direction, both head from the airport to Faro's beach.

➡ A taxi to central Faro costs €10, or €11 at night and weekends.

➡ There are numerous car-hire firms to choose from at arrivals.

By Train

➡ The Algarve is easily accessed by **train** (www.cp.pt) from Lisbon and further afield, with services to Faro, Lagos and other towns.

➡ From Lisbon's Gare do Oriente (Oriente Station) to Faro there are five departures daily (€22.20, three to 3½ hours).

By Bus

➡ The Algarve is connected to the rest of Portugal by a comprehensive network of intercity buses. There are also connections from Huelva and Seville in Spain to Faro.

➡ Buses from Lisbon to Faro (€20, 3¼ to 4½ hours) are run by **Renex** (www.renex.pt), **Eva Transportes** (📞 289 899 700; www.eva-bus.com) and **Rede Expressos** (📞 707 223 344; www.rede-expressos.pt). These companies also run to Lagos and other Algarve destinations.

Getting Around

Bicycle

☑ **Best for...** Exploring the inland areas away from the busy coastal roads.

➡ Distances aren't great, so cycling is a good way of getting around.

➡ Plot your coastal routes to avoid the main roads, which can get very busy. You'll find less traffic in the hilly, but beautiful, interior.

➡ There are hire places in nearly every coastal town. Think €10 to €20 for a day, or €50 to €80 per week.

➡ A lot of Algarve villages have cobbled streets and wheel-chasing dogs – beware!

Bus

☑ **Best for...** Regular departures and access to both coastal and inland areas.

➡ A good bus network runs along the Algarve coast and to Loulé. The west coast and inland areas have more limited services. The four main companies servicing the area are **Eva Transportes** (📞 289 899 700; www.eva-bus.com), **Rede Expressos** (📞 707 223 344; www.rede-expressos.pt), **Renex** (www.renex.pt) and **Frota Azul** (www.frotazul-algarve.pt).

➡ Bus service slows down considerably on weekends – particularly on Sunday.

Car & Motorcycle

☑ **Best for...** Going wherever you want at your own pace.

➡ Car hire is very popular. Prices are competitive, so use online brokers, but beware of hidden extras.

➡ Many companies also hire mopeds, scooters and motorcycles, with delivery to transport terminals an option.

→ You usually need to be at least 21 to hire a car.

→ Remember to drive on the right.

→ Some motorways are automatically tolled, so get a device with your hire car, put your credit card in a machine as you drive in overland or buy a voucher. See www.portugaltolls.pt for more.

Train

☑ **Best for...** Hassle-free tripping along the south coast.

→ A line runs along the Algarve's southern coast from Lagos to Faro and east to Vila Real de Santo António, near the Spanish border, making the train a good option for hops along the southern beaches.

→ Slow regional trains run the route. Sample journeys include Faro to Tavira (€3.15, 40 minutes, 11 to 15 daily), and Lagos to Faro (€7.30, 1¾ hours, eight to nine daily).

Essential Information

Business Hours

☑ **Top Tip** Things tend to shut down for an hour or two around lunchtime, so do as the locals do and sit down for a meal.

Banks 8.30am to 3pm Monday to Friday

Bars 7pm to 2am

Cafes 9am to 7pm

Clubs 11pm to 4am Thursday to Saturday

Restaurants Noon to 3pm and 7pm to 10pm

Shops 9.30am to noon and 2pm to 7pm Monday to Friday, 10am to 1pm Saturday

Electricity

230V/50Hz

230V/50Hz

Emergencies

Dial ☎112 for any emergency.

Money

☑ **Top Tip** Credit cards are accepted in smarter hotels and restaurants, but are of little use in budget places.

→ Portugal uses the euro (€). There are notes of 5, 10, 20, 50, 100, 200 and 500 euros, and coins of 1, 2, 5, 10, 20 and 50 cents, and €1 and €2.

→ ATMs are widespread. Check to see what your home bank will charge you for withdrawals.

→ There are plenty of exchange offices and banks to change cash.

➡ Tipping in restaurants is not expected, but appreciated. Locals leave around 2% to 5%; 10% is generous. Upmarket places may add a service charge of up to 15%. There's no need to tip in bars except for table service.

Public Holidays

Some former holidays have been cancelled due to tough economic times, but are scheduled to return a few years down the track.

New Year's Day 1 January

Carnaval Tuesday Tuesday before Ash Wednesday (February/March)

Good Friday March/April

Easter Monday March/ April

Liberty Day 25 April (celebrating the 1974 revolution)

Labour Day 1 May

Portugal Day 10 June (also known as Camões and Communities Day)

Feast of the Assumption 15 August

All Saints' Day 1 November

Feast of the Immaculate Conception 8 December

Christmas Day 25 December

Safe Travel

This is Portugal's most touristed area, and petty theft is prevalent. Never leave valuables unattended in the car or on the beach.

Swimmers should beware of temperamental coast conditions, especially on the west coast. Most of the Algarve's beaches have lifeguards daily in the summer months, when flags indicate their presence. Green flags mean the water is safe, yellow mean you should enter with caution, and red signify it's unsafe. A chequered flag means the beach is temporarily unsupervised.

Telephone Services

➡ **Codes and calls** To call Portugal from abroad, the country code is 📞351. All domestic numbers have nine digits, and there are no area codes. Most public phones accept phonecards only (available at most news-stands).

➡ **Roaming** Roaming charges within the EU are being phased out, so for EU residents it's reasonably cheap to use your own mobile in Portugal these days, though data can be more expensive.

➡ **SIM cards** Major operators are MEO, Vodafone and NOS. All sell prepaid SIM cards that you can use as long as your phone is unlocked. There are good packages available that include calls, data and SMS.

Tourist Information

➡ The Algarve's tourist website (www.visitalgarve. pt) is excellent; download brochures, maps and various publications.

Money-Saving Tips

➡ At lunchtime, restaurants often serve a daily special (*prato do dia*), usually great value at €5 to €9.

➡ The **Passe Turístico** (Tourist Pass; www.eva-bus.com) gives you unlimited travel on Eva and Frota Azul buses for three (€29.10) or seven (€36.25) days.

➡ If you're near the Spanish border, nip across to fill up with petrol; it's usually around €0.25 per litre cheaper.

➡ Locally managed *postos de turismo* (tourist offices; usually signposted *urismo*) offer good multilingual map-brochures and varying degrees of help. Maps for other areas cost €0.50, while a range of in-depth spiral-bound guides (€7, or a free download) offer extra information on activities such as golf, birdwatching and hiking.

➡ Turismo de Portugal, the country's national tourist board, also operates a website: www.visitportugal. om.

➡ Some useful tourist offices are listed here or visit www.visitalgarve.pt:

Aljezur (☑282 998 229; Rua 5 de Abril 62; ☺9am-6pm ue-Thu, 9am-1pm & 2-6pm ri-Mon)

aro (Map p30, C4; Rua da Misericórdia 8; ☺9am-1pm 2-6pm)

agos (Map p82, C2; ☑282 63 031; Praça Gil Eanes; ☺9am-7pm Jul & Aug, to om Easter-Jun & Sep, to 5pm ct-Easter)

oulé (Map p54, E3; ☑289 63 900; Av 25 de Abril 9; ☺9am-1pm & 2-6pm Tue-Sat)

Monchique (Map p74, B3; ☑282 911 189; Largo de São

The Couvert

Throughout Portugal, waiters bring bread, olives and other items when you sit down; this is called the *couvert* and is never free; it costs from €0.50 to €8 (it's often itemised), depending on the place. If you don't want it, send part or all of it away.

Sebastião; ☺9am-1pm & 2-6pm Tue-Sat)

Sagres (Map p96, C2; ☑282 624 873; www.cm-viladobispo. pt; Rua Comandante Matoso; ☺9am-1pm & 2-6pm Tue-Sat, extended hours in summer)

Silves (Map p64, C3; Largo do Município; ☺9am-1pm & 2-5pm Mon-Fri)

Tavira (Map p44, B3; ☑281 322 511; Praça da República 5; ☺9am-6pm Mon-Fri, 9am-1pm & 2-6pm Sat & Sun, to 7pm Jul & Aug).

Travellers with Disabilities

➡ The Algarve is better than the rest of Portugal for disabled needs, but awareness is nonetheless limited. Public offices and agencies are required to provide access and facilities for people with disabilities.

➡ Faro airport has accessible toilets.

➡ Dedicated parking spaces are widely available. The EU parking card entitles visitors to the same street-parking concessions given to disabled residents.

➡ Newer and larger hotels tend to have adapted rooms, though the facilities may not be up to scratch; ask detailed questions before booking.

➡ Most camping grounds have accessible toilets and some hostels have disabled facilities.

Visas

➡ EU nationals don't need a visa for any length of stay in Portugal and can enter with their national identity card.

➡ Those from many other countries, including Canada, New Zealand, the USA, Japan and Australia can stay for up to 90 days without a visa.

➡ Others, including nationals of South Africa, need a visa, which is valid for all other European countries in the Schengen agreement.

Language

Most sounds in Portuguese are also found in English. The exceptions are the nasal vowels (represented in our pronunciation guides by '*ng*' after the vowel), pronounced as if you're trying to make the sound through your nose; and the strongly rolled *r* (represented by '*rr*' in our pronunciation guides). Also note that the symbol '*zh*' sounds like the 's' in 'pleasure'. Keeping these few points in mind and reading the pronunciation guides as if they were English, you'll be understood just fine. The stressed syllables are indicated with italics.

To enhance your trip with a phrasebook, visit **lonelyplanet.com**.

Basics

Hello.
Olá.   o·*laa*

Goodbye.
Adeus.   a·de·*oosh*

How are you?
Como está?   ko·moo *shtaa*

Fine, and you?
Bem, e você?   beng e vo·*se*

Please.
Por favor.   poor fa·*vor*

Thank you.
Obrigado. (m)   o·*bree*·gaa·doo
Obrigada. (f)   o·*bree*·gaa·da

Excuse me.
Faz favor.   faash fa·*vor*

Sorry.
Desculpe.   desh·*kool*·pe

Yes./No.
Sim./Não.   seeng/nowng

I don't understand.
Não entendo.   nowng eng·*teng*·doo

Do you speak English?
Fala inglês?   faa·la eeng·*glesh*

Eating & Drinking

..., please.   ..., *por favor.* ... poor fa·*vor*

A coffee   *Um café*   oong ka·*fe*

A table   *Uma mesa*   oo·ma me·za
  for two   *para duas*   pa·ra doo·ash
                 pessoas   pe·so·ash

Two beers   *Dois*   doysh
              cervejas   ser·ve·zhash

I'm a vegetarian.
Eu sou   e·oo soh
vegetariano/   ve·zhe·a·ree·a·noo/
vegetariana. (m/f)   ve·zhe·a·ree·a·na

Cheers!
Saúde!   sa·oo·de

That was delicious!
Isto estava   eesh·too shtaa·va
delicioso!   de·lee·see·o·zoo

The bill, please.
A conta, por favor.   a kong·ta poor fa·vo

Shopping

I'd like to buy ...
Queria   ke·ree·a
comprar ...   kong·praar ...

I'm just looking.
Estou só a ver.   shtoh so a ver

How much is it?
Quanto custa?   kwang·too koosh·ta

It's too expensive.
Está muito
caro.
shtaa mweeng·too
kaa·roo

Can you lower the price?
Pode baixar
o preço?
po·de bai·shaar
oo pre·soo

Emergencies

Help!
Socorro!
soo·ko·rroo

Call a doctor!
Chame um
médico!
shaa·me oong
me·dee·koo

Call the police!
Chame a
polícia!
shaa·me a
poo·lee·sya

I'm sick.
Estou doente.
shtoh doo·eng·te

I'm lost.
Estou perdido. (m)
Estou perdida. (f)
shtoh per·dee·doo
shtoh per·dee·da

Where's the toilet?
Onde é a casa de
banho?
ong·de e a kaa·za de
ba·nyoo

Time & Numbers

What time is it?
Que horas são?
kee o·rash sowng

It's (10) o'clock.
São (dez) horas.
sowng (desh) o·rash

Half past (10).
(Dez) e meia.
(desh) e may·a

morning	manhã	ma·nyang
afternoon	tarde	taar·de
evening	noite	noy·te
yesterday	ontem	ong·teng

today	hoje	o·zhe
tomorrow	amanhã	aa·ma·nyang
1	um	oong
2	dois	doysh
3	três	tresh
4	quatro	kwaa·troo
5	cinco	seeng·koo
6	seis	saysh
7	sete	se·te
8	oito	oy·too
9	nove	no·ve
10	dez	desh

Transport & Directions

Where's ...?
Onde é ...?
ong·de e ...

What's the address?
Qual é o
endereço?
kwaal e oo
eng·de·re·soo

Can you show me (on the map)?
Pode-me
mostrar
(no mapa)?
po·de·me
moosh·traar
(noo maa·pa)

When's the next bus?
Quando é que sai
o próximo
autocarro?
kwang·doo e ke sai
oo pro·see·moo
ow·to·kaa·rroo

I want to go to ...
Queria ir a ...
ke·ree·a eer a ...

Does it stop at ...?
Pára em ...?
paa·ra eng ...

Please stop here.
Por favor pare
aqui.
poor fa·vor paa·re
a·kee

Behind the Scenes

Send Us Your Feedback

We love to hear from travellers – your comments help make our books better. We read every word, and we guarantee that your feedback goes straight to the authors. Visit **lonelyplanet.com/contact** to submit your updates and suggestions.

Note: We may edit, reproduce and incorporate your comments in Lonely Planet products such as guidebooks, websites and digital products, so let us know if you don't want your comments reproduced or your name acknowledged. For a copy of our privacy policy visit lonelyplanet.com/privacy.

Andy Symington's Thanks

Numerous people were generous with information, but I owe particular thanks for hospitality and other favours to James and Penny Symington, Rupert and Anne Symington, David and Sara Jane Symington, António Valente, Catrin Egerton, Wil Peters, Ricardo Feijóo, Miguel Amaral, João Valente and Jose Eliseo Vázquez González. A big *obrigado* also to Jo Cooke and Lorna Parkes for being great editors to work with.

Acknowledgments

Cover photo: Carvoeiro, Portugal. Sabine Lubenow/Corbis ©
Contents photo: (pp4–5): Fortaleza de Sagres, Portugal. Miguel Angel Garin/ Getty ©

This Book

This 1st edition of Lonely Planet's *Pocket Algarve* was researched and written by Andy Symington.

This guidebook was produced by the following:

Destination Editor Lorna Parkes

Product Editors Martine Power, Amanda Williamson
Senior Cartographers Mark Griffiths, Anthony Phelan
Book Designers Mazzy Prinsep, Wendy Wright
Assisting Book Designer Jessica Rose

Assisting Editors Charlotte Orr, Saralinda Turner
Cover Researcher Campbell McKenzie
Thanks to Sasha Baskett, Jo Cooke, Andi Jones, Jenna Myers, Catherine Naghten, Karyn Noble, Julie Sheridan, Angela Tinson, Tony Wheeler

Index

See also separate subindexes for:

🍴 **Eating p142**

🍷 **Drinking p143**

🎭 **Entertainment p143**

🛍 **Shopping p143**

Our Writer

Andy Symington

Though he hails from Australia, Andy's great-grandfather emigrated to Portugal in the 19th century and that side of his family still calls the country home. This connection means that he has been a frequent visitor to the country since birth, and now nips across the border very frequently from his home in Spain. He loves the Algarve's compact dimensions, scope for outdoor activity and fabulous beaches. Andy has authored and co-authored numerous Lonely Planet and other guidebooks.

Published by Lonely Planet Publications Pty Ltd
ABN 36 005 607 983
1st edition – December 2015
ISBN 978 1 74360 711 4
© Lonely Planet 2015   Photographs © as indicated 2015
10 9 8 7 6 5 4
Printed in Singapore